FRAGMENTS OF REALITY

Tony Flannery CSsR

Fragments of Reality

COLLECTED WRITINGS

the columba press

First published in 2008 by
the columba press
55A Spruce Avenue, Stillorgan Industrial Park,
Blackrock, Co Dublin

Cover by Bill Bolger
Origination by The Columba Press
Printed in Ireland by ColourBooks Ltd, Dublin

ISBN 978-1-85607-624-1

Thematic Index

Introduction

The collection of articles in this book was all written within the past ten years, almost all since the turn of the century. Many of them first saw the light of day in *Reality* magazine. They cover a variety of topics, to do with church, religion and society. During those years I worked as a member of the Redemptorist Mission Team which comprised lay people and clergy. We travelled to parishes in all four provinces, and many of the dioceses in the country.

The past ten years have been interesting times in both church and society. For the church it was the time when the initial heat of the sex abuse crisis began to wane, and we gradually got it into some sort of perspective. The shock of the early years was replaced by some sense of realism, and church people gradually faced up to what had happened, and put measures in place that might provide more protection in the future. None of this has been easy, and the response has varied greatly from parish to parish, and more so from diocese to diocese. But generally I think it is fair to say that the church has been more proactive in putting child protection structures in place than many other institutions. We also managed to raise the issue of some false accusations against priests, and now I think there is a healthier, more sceptical attitude around than in the early years, though we still have some way to go in this area. It is still true, I believe, that a person who makes an accusation against a priest or religious is more likely to get substantial compensation than if it was a member of a profession that is protected by a trades union.

During these years we have seen a continued and steady decline in church attendance, though you will see from the articles that there is no uniform pattern to this, and that attendance at the religious events that we Redemptorists conduct is still remarkably high – though it must also be recognised that the response to the parish mission/novena is definitely not what it used to be. Depending on my experience in the different parishes, some articles in this collection demonstrate a certain pessimism about the future, while others are quite upbeat. There are times when I have felt that we are in a healthier state than ever before, in the sense that those who attend church today largely do so because they *want* to be there. The days of coercion, either religious or social, are gone. In that context it is quite remarkable how many still show an interest. There have been other times when I felt that the slide would continue irrevocably until we became like the continent, with most of our churches standing empty. The next generation will tell the decisive tale on that issue.

The other major area of decline for the church has been in candidates for the priesthood. This, of course, has been happening for about thirty years now, but at this stage it has reached crisis point. The actual number of priests in this country hasn't fallen dramatically, since it continues to be inflated by the return of retired missionaries from foreign countries, but it is the age structure that tells the real story. The average age for the clergy in Ireland, at this time, must be close to seventy. More and more parishes are now being staffed by one elderly priest, who barely manages to supply the basic services. It is in this area more than any other that I feel the church has particularly failed over the past ten years. The same rigid rules apply for qualification for ministry. To be a priest one has to be male, and willing to make a life-long commitment to celibacy. There is only a very slight effort being made to face the reality of what is happening. By and large the authorities continue to move around their depleted resources in a futile effort to fill all the gaps and keep the show on the road. It is here more than in any other area that the lack of leadership is being shown up in the church. Our bishops continue to be in thrall to the slightest whim of the Vatican, and show no capacity to think for themselves. There is no indication that they are a cohesive national body with a shared vision. Extensive lip service has been given to the involvement of the laity, but in practice very little is being done, and priests are still allowed to act in a dictatorial fashion without any repercussion from, and indeed in some cases with the approval of, their bishop. So I have met with numerous instances where enthusiastic lay involvement in a parish was summarily scattered by a new parish priest. This sort of thing has led to a widespread disillusionment among the laity, who increasingly do not see the point in giving of their time and expertise when all the power remains in the hands of the priest, who can ignore them as he chooses.

In this, as in so many other ways, we in the church are suffering from the disastrous appointments policy pursued by the Vatican under the long reign of Pope John Paul II. Orthodoxy rather than ability was the guiding principle for the choices that were made, and as a consequence we have had many men in positions of authority who had neither the aptitude nor the capacity for the job. Hans Küng, in a recent interview with Paul Vallely in *The Tablet*, (to coincide with his eightieth birthday), put it like this: 'The heritage of Pope John Paul II is many mediocre bishops, some absolute failures and very many incompetent people just obeying Rome's orders. This is a very big problem. It's a dangerous policy just to appoint people who toe the party line.'

The last issue which has bedevilled the church during this period is the continued denial of any meaningful role for women in ministry. How much longer can this policy be sustained? We must be the last institution in the Western World that continues to uphold such blatant discrimination against women. I don't have any doubt that there is no theological or scriptural basis for this position, but that it is purely a social and institutional construct hiding a fairly barefaced and primitive desire for male domination. At the moment the Irish Church is introducing lay deacons, of course restricted to males. I hope this is not supported by the people. No man should allow his name to go forward for a position that excludes women.

The church is paying a big price for this rigid, discriminative policy in relation to ministry. Hans Küng in the same interview put it very well where, speaking about his native Switzerland, he made two basic points which I think are significant. The first one is that the parish structure is collapsing because it continues to be identified with the presence of the priest. In reality the parish is the priest rather than the people, so when there is no priest there is no parish. Küng says this is disastrous. His second point is a more difficult one to write about (there is always the danger of being labelled homophobic), but Küng says that a direct result of the celibacy rule in the church is the high percentage of gay men in the priesthood. 'The irony is that because of the celibacy law homosexuals are attracted to seminaries in disproportionate numbers. This creates a very unhealthy atmosphere which must be changed.' I agree with Küng in this. It is not to suggest that homosexuals do not make as good priests as heterosexuals, but if we have disproportionate numbers among priests there is clearly a problem.

These past ten years have seen the Celtic Tiger sweep across the land, bringing previously undreamed of prosperity. Observing all this from my perspective as a preacher of the Christian gospel I became aware of certain negative trends.

There was an almost adolescent glee about the way we as a nation reacted to our newfound wealth. We quickly forgot the lessons of the past and began to spend as if there was no tomorrow. To a fair extent we also seemed to believe that prosperity would solve all our problems and make us happy in a way that we had never been happy before. We undoubtedly became greedy, individualistic and our values and standards of morality dropped. People used means to achieve wealth that would have been frowned on in previous generations, but were now lauded. Social Darwinism thrived. Many had little or no time for religion, seeing it as a killjoy in the midst of all the fun. Often during the ten years the quote from T.S. Eliot went through my mind: 'In times of prosperity people neglect the temple.' One of the results of our obsession with economic gain is a gradual breakdown in community. Increasingly people are not involved with their neighbours, even in rural areas, and the upshot of this is that life is lonelier and more isolated for many people. As houses get bigger, more luxurious and ostentatious, the inhabitants spend less and less time in them, because their lives have become more busy and stress-filled. Success is measured in material terms, and the drive to get to the top of the ladder leaves many casualties along the way. So our society has become more harsh and ruthless, a much less kind environment for the weak, the vulnerable and the old.

Our politicians have come through a difficult ten years, during which their standing in the community has suffered. They are less well regarded now than in the past. Some of this is a result of the behaviour of certain of their members, who were clearly involved in corrupt practices to do with planning and rezoning of land. But not all of them are corrupt, and the tendency of people and media to presume that they are all the same has been very destructive. Respect and belief in the democratic institutions are essential for any society, and it worries me to see so much cynicism around.

This brings me to the final point I wish to make here on the past ten years. The quality of media coverage and comment has greatly disimproved. This applies both to the spoken and written media.

In its coverage and comment it has become superficial and sensational. This trend is not just an Irish phenomenon, and of course there are some honourable exceptions to it, but it is a shame to see it happening. Most media outlets now seem to be driven by agendas, and the facts are presented in such a way as to fit that agenda, with little concern for the truth. A healthy society needs wise people who have an ability to stand back and reflect sensibly and intelligently on what is happening. Those voices are being drowned out in Ireland today. Regrettably, rational, thoughtful comment tends to be balanced and fair, not sensational and dogmatic, and so it does not get much of a hearing in modern life.

The articles in this book are my effort to redress the balance by seeking to make some attempt at fair-minded and even-handed comment on society and church in Ireland today.

A Balanced Reaction

Ann teaches junior infants in a primary school. She has taken a year out to work with us, the Redemptorist Mission team stationed in Esker, Co Galway. We are glad to have her, for a number of reasons. Apart from being a beautiful singer, and bringing many other talents to our work, she also has a dramatic impact on the average age of the team, reducing it from the low sixties to the low forties. Her presence on the altar is some slight gesture towards gender balance in our otherwise male clerical team.

Recently we were celebrating Mass with a primary school group on one of our missions. At least I was doing the ministerial part of the event, while Ann looked after the rest. What a pleasure it was to be able to sit back and leave it to her rather than trying to communicate with a group who were a couple of generations younger than me. At the end of the Mass she moved down among the infants. They flocked around her. In a totally unselfconscious way she straightened their caps, zipped up their jackets, and hugs were exchanged while they chatted away. Physical contact was the order of the day.

As I sat watching her from the relative safety of the sanctuary it came home to me what a change the child sexual abuse issue has brought about. A slight pat on the head is the limit of the physical contact I would have with a child now, and even that would only be attempted in a very public area. That is not because I am a priest, but because I am a man. Being a priest probably adds to the constraint at the moment, but the fundamental reason for my reticence with children is my maleness. It is increasingly regarded as inappropriate for a man to have any physical contact with a child, unless it happens to be his own son or daughter. There are guidelines to be observed, and records to be kept, which effectively destroy any possibility of spontaneity between us.

I think in all of this we as a society have over-reacted in our response to the child abuse problem. By effectively depriving our children of the possibility of appropriate male intimacy and affection, we may end up doing more damage to a larger number than was caused by the problem we are trying to solve. This imbalance in our reaction is brought about by a naïvety in modern Irish life, and particularly the media presentation of it. There seems to be a belief that we can actually eradicate wrong behaviour if only we put the proper structures and sufficient sanctions in place. This is one of the many ways in which we are suffering from the absence of a sensible and balanced philosophy of life, now that most of the influential sections of society have rejected the Christian interpretation. Christianity tells us that the world, and every human person, is involved in a struggle between good and evil, and that struggle will continue until the end of time. As a politician recently explained, in a show of admirable self-understanding, 'I am fifty per cent good and fifty per cent bad; I hope that by the time I come to die I will have tilted the balance in favour of the good.' That is the best we can hope for in this world, and after that we trust in the goodness of God to make up for our failure.

But those who don't have a religious philosophy are left with human devices to try to sort out the problem of evil. They think that proper laws and structures will eradicate problems, for example that of child abuse. They paint the child abuser as a 'beast', as 'vile' and 'subhuman'. In that way they distance themselves from him. He is an outsider, and they have nothing in common with him. They fail to recognise the extraordinary complexity of the human person, and how each one of us contains within ourselves the capacity for outstanding goodness, but also the possibility of great evil. As one old man said to me recently, 'In the course of my lifetime I have come to know a number of convicted child abusers. The strange thing is that in so many ways they were good and lovely people.' In the Christian understanding of the human person that makes perfect sense. But to those who wish to brand abusers as inhuman beasts it is incomprehensible.

Trying to retain a sense of balance in dealing with the problems of life is very important. Balance comes from having a philosophy that gives us a clear understanding of life, and of ourselves, and being realistic about what is possible. Armed with this knowledge, we will not go over the top about any one issue, and lose perspective about the long-term consequences of our actions.

A Hard Time to be A Parent

I have great sympathy for today's generation of young parents, and in particular young mothers. They seem to me to be facing challenges that are new and more difficult than any that have gone before. In this article, I will highlight three of the major ones.

Infertility would appear to be on the increase. As an older unmarried man with no children of my own, I have only the smallest appreciation of the ache that a woman can feel to hold her own child in her arms, and the pain that must be associated with infertility. When I enquired from a friend of mine, who is much more versed in these matters than I, why infertility is on the increase, she said that it is a complex question, but there are two obvious contributory factors. The first is that women are getting married and having children at a later age. Many young women now consider the late twenties or early thirties as the appropriate time to begin having children. They want to build a career, and maybe travel the world, first. But by this age they are already well past the time of peak fertility. The second reason my friend gave is the long-term use of the contraceptive pill. Some girls are already on the pill in their mid teens, many because they are sexually active, or their doctor might prescribe the pill in order to regulate the cycle or ease the pain of menstruation. 'Long years of using a drug to interfere with the natural human processes is bound to have an effect,' my friend said.

Having had a child or children, the couple are then faced with the second big problem, the question of childcare. In the case of most young couples today, both father and mother work outside the home. I have often asked couples if it is unavoidable that both work. They assure me it is, and they describe their situation as being caught in an economic bind which forces this particular lifestyle on them. When I enquire if a simpler lifestyle is an option, they tell me it is not. I know that some people say that part of the problem is that they want to have everything immediately, and are not willing to wait for many of the accessories of modern life until they can afford them. I don't know, but I would imagine that if both parents are working, it is essential that they also share responsibility for the running of the home and the upbringing of the children. Those I have spoken to assure me that most young fathers are quite good in this area. If this is true, it is a great credit to them. To have changed so dramatically from previous generations of fathers is quite an achievement.

The third challenge for young couples is holding a marriage relationship together. I wonder where they find time for each other. Having spent the day at work, and the evening trying to make the house habitable and attending to the children, how can they have either time or energy for each other? It must be very difficult. They belong to a generation that have been taught to expect much from a relationship, in terms of meeting their own needs. But when the children come, the priorities of a relationship have to change, and it must be hard, especially for the man, to adjust. Where there are small children, it is their needs that become more important than their parents'. While not for a moment taking away from the courageous lives of so many single parents, I think it is true that the best environment for the rearing of a child is a home where both parents are present and involved with the children. In recent times we have tended to deride the notion of two people staying together for the sake of the children. I know that where a relationship has become seriously destructive, a couple must separate. But in the more common case of a couple who are not getting on very well, but where there isn't violence or serious addictive behaviour, I think it is a good and courageous thing for them to stay together in order to give the children the best possible upbringing they can.

All in all I don't envy this generation of young parents. They have got more money and possessions, more beautiful houses and cars, than ever before. But the human price they pay is very high.

A Moral Code for Today

There was shock on the *Late, Late Show* when the woman rang in to describe the scenes she had witnessed outside the disco when she went to pick up her twelve-year-old daughter at the end of the evening. To use the old phrase, what she described would make the most decadent days of the Roman Empire seem like *Outlook*. We have no reason to believe that she, or indeed many others who describe scenes of sexual depravity among our young people, are exaggerating. On the other hand, I work a good bit with young people on our missions, and they are always at pains to point out that the media highlight the extreme cases, and then paint everyone with the same brush. I know from recent experience as a priest what that is like!

But still there is clearly a problem. Somewhere along the way moral guidance seems to have broken down, and at least some of our young people are left without any real sense of what is appropriate, what type of behaviour is wise or foolish – indeed, to put it in the traditional language that does not tend to be favoured today, what is right or wrong. Why has this happened?

Many commentators have said over recent years that Ireland could be in trouble as a result of the waning influence of the Catholic Church. This conclusion was based on the belief that the church was the dominant moral teacher, almost to the exclusion of any other. In most other European countries people gave allegiance to secular codes of decency and moral behaviour. Here in Ireland Catholic morality reigned. When this no longer holds sway, what is there to replace it? Some say that we are left with something of a moral wasteland. Which is probably not a bad description of what we are told is happening in certain aspects of our young people's social interaction.

I know that the church is not free from blame in all of this. It has brought a lot of its misfortune on its own head. Apart from the disastrous effects of the child abuse scandals, we have also done a very poor job in presenting the Christian teaching on relationships and sexuality. I think it is not unfair to say that we have presented what is a very positive and life-affirming set of principles as something negative, restrictive and life-denying. Christ gave us a teaching that is full of wisdom and common sense about life and people. Our desire to control people's lives has led to a warped presentation of it.

As a result we have been pilloried, ridiculed and ultimately dismissed as having nothing useful to say on the matter. There has been a certain adolescent glee about the way writers and commentators generally have hoed into the church in recent years. Clearly they were driven by all sorts of hang-ups and resentments from the past. Personal agendas were obvious, and objective comment was at a premium. This was understandable for a certain period of time. But now we should be well past that phase. Unfortunately we are not. The same old tired and ultimately superficial diatribes against the church are being trotted out endlessly. It is time we realised that the situation has moved far beyond this. In other words, it is time we grew up and faced the reality of today, and the urgent problems we have to deal with.

Where are we going to find what I would call a moral code, or for those who find that type of language too redolent of past oppressions, a commonly accepted set of standards about decency and right behaviour between people? Who are the wise people in society today who can guide us in this direction? There is no doubt about the urgency of the task. We are doing a frightful injustice to our young people if we fail to give them guidance, and provide appropriate boundaries for them as they grow up. Society will yield a disastrous harvest. So let us all leave the old hurts and grievances behind us. We have aired them sufficiently. And give our energy to solving the problems of today.

Can the church play any useful part in this debate about acceptable standards for modern Ireland? I am not sure. In order to do so we would need to be very open and flexible, and we haven't shown ourselves proficient in either quality in recent times. If we continue to make big issues, and hold rigid lines, on particular aspects of sexual morality, our voice will not be heard. We will continue to be regarded as irrelevant, and rightly so. We have to earn our right to be heard again. We can do this by focusing anew on the wisdom of Christ's teaching, while leaving people the freedom and flexibility to work out the details in their own lives.

A New Freedom

I notice that people generally assume that my work, conducting parish missions and novenas, is considerably more difficult in the present climate in the Irish church. And in some ways they are right. Standing up day after day in front of people, when the newspapers, radio and television are full of stories of priests abusing children, is not easy. You wonder should you be addressing the issue, and if so, what is there to say? And inevitably you are conscious, in any dealings with children, of being watched, and maybe even slightly under suspicion. And yet these past months I have been involved in some of the best missions I have experienced in all my years at the work. The crowds have been large and enthusiastic, and there was a sense of solidarity, and of community, that have been both satisfying and hopeful. It is as if people have sensed that in the current crisis in the church, we need to come together like never before, and that in coming together we draw strength and life from each other.

Down through the years I have often preached about how Christianity is a community religion, not something we practise as individuals, but together. In the past few months I have come to an understanding of that in a much deeper way. I believe there is also a realisation among ordinary Catholics that the 'official' church, meaning the priests and bishops, has somehow lost its way, is unable to adequately handle the situation, and they are slowly rising out of generations of lethargy and starting to take responsibility. That is exciting to see.

I also sense a new freedom about the church. The boundaries are breaking down in many areas. There is more ease between priest and people, now that many of the false illusions about the holiness and wisdom of the priest have been shattered. A more ordinary, human relationship can develop. And the priest, having been stripped of his authority, can relate to the people on a level of equality. There is less concern with orthodoxy, and with strict observance of rules and regulations. Much of that has been put into its proper perspective by the more serious matters we have had to deal with.

Of course I am well aware that not all priests or people are able to adjust to this new reality, and some are clinging on to the old ways and attitudes. But there is real change happening, and it is good to see. So, I find myself being more hopeful than all our present difficulties might warrant.

Why is it that we priests and bishops have proved so inadequate at this time? The particular failure on our part that I find hard to understand is our failure to handle the public dimension of our difficulties. Among the body of Irish clergy there are many brilliant men, highly educated. Over the years we have had the services of people like Barry Baker, Bunny Carr, Tom Savage and Terry Prone, to teach us the skills of communication and how to deal with the media. Endless courses have been done. I know many will say that the media are out to get the church, and that, for instance, a bishop appearing on one of the main TV programmes would be the equivalent of the Christians facing the lions in the Colosseum. I don't agree. I know there are unfair elements in the media, and some who are more interested in a sensational story than in the truth. But any institution today needs to have a highly skilled public relations team. The unwillingness of our bishops, again with one or two exceptions, to allow themselves to face public scrutiny, is no longer a luxury we can afford. I do know, of course, that many of them are totally inadequate when it comes to dealing with the media, and that is part of the serious lack of leadership we are suffering.

In all of this we are again paying the price of our obsession with orthodoxy in the time of Pope John Paul II. There are priests I can think of, some of them well known, who would be excellent spokespeople. But the church has not used them, because it could not guarantee that they would always give out the official line. We have got to learn from our present troubles that a spokesperson who is only capable of parroting official answers is of no use at all. Let us trust the people of ability among us, lay and clergy, women and men, and give them the freedom to speak the truth as they see it. It is only in that way we will begin to regain our credibility.

A not so gentle Jesus

'Gentle Jesus, meek and mild', as the old children's prayer rhyme goes. When he was criticising the religious leaders of his day, Jesus was anything but meek and mild. Addressing 'some Pharisees and teachers of the Law' in Matthew's Gospel, he says: 'You hypocrites! How right Isaiah was when he prophesied about you. These people, says God, honour me with their words, but their heart is really far away from me. It is no use for them to worship me, because they teach man-made rules as though they were my laws.'

In Luke's Gospel he fulminates against the teachers of the Law: 'How terrible for you, teachers of the Law. You have kept the key that opens the door to the house of knowledge; you yourselves will not go in, and you stop those who are trying to go in.'

He antagonised the religious leaders so much that it was they who fomented the agitation that led to his execution. Clearly a great deal of organised religion at the time did not greatly impress Jesus, and equally they were not impressed by him. I often ask myself if he came back today what he would make of all the different expressions of religious belief we have in the world now. Let me guess.

I don't think he would be impressed by the multiplicity of Christian churches, all claiming to be the true church that he founded, and the many points of law and doctrine that we quarrel over. I can't imagine him devoting too much energy to the exact meaning of the word 'transubstantiation', or getting caught up in a debate about ministers of one denomination being more truly priests and descendants of the apostles that those of another. I suspect that he would quickly cut to the heart of his teaching, and tell us to get on with it, reminding us of one of his core statements: 'By this shall everyone know that you are my disciples, if you love one another.'

I don't think he would feel at home in the Vatican. It would be too big, too pompous and too bureaucratic for him. I cannot see him dressing up in all the ceremonial robes. He would more likely be found in jeans and tee shirt, out on the streets mixing with the common people. If he wandered into a Catholic library and saw the shelves overflowing with books of theology and law, he would probably tell us we have made it all too complicated. He might even criticise us, as he did the Scribes of his time, for laying impossible burdens on people's shoulders. Or maybe he would say, as he did to the rich young man, that we should sell all that we have, big churches, palaces, monasteries, the lot, and give the money to the poor. He might tell us that only then would we be able to follow him. And if we objected that we needed these possessions for our long term security, the likely answer would be that we should trust him instead.

I cannot imagine that he would be comfortable with the movement towards fundamentalism that we are witnessing in various religions in the world today. When he would hear apparently devout Christians and Muslims speaking in the name of God and calling each other evil, I suspect words like 'whited sepulchre' and 'hypocrite' would be heard again. There is no way that he would justify wars fought in the name of God. He would surely have harsh words to say to the form of Protestant Evangelism that is so strong in the United States at the moment. He would approve of their stand in favour of the lives of unborn children, but point out the contradiction between that and their support for war and capital punishment. He would surely want the richest and most powerful nation in the world to use its enormous resources to eliminate poverty and hunger rather than piling up weapons of not just mass, but total destruction. I suspect that hunger and poverty would be the issues more than any other that would exercise him. We would all feel the lash of his tongue over the dreadful inequality in the world. Modern versions of the story of the rich man and Lazarus lying at his gate would no doubt be told, with an equally strong warning of the destruction that awaits us unless we repent and change.

I'm sure he would have much more to say. In his day the Pharisees, the Scribes, the teachers of the Law, with a few exceptions, did not listen to him. Would the religious leaders of today, we priests, the bishops, ministers of other Christian churches, be any more open? Probably not. We would have too much emotional, personal and financial investment in the *status quo*. We would resent someone who would try to get us to see things in a new way. I wonder would we crucify him.

A Possible Way Forward for the Church

I suppose it is understandable that someone in my position, a preacher of missions and novenas, would regularly find himself engaged in discussions about the future of the Catholic Church in Ireland. How are we going to deal with falling numbers in our churches, with the increasingly severe shortage of priests, with low morale, and all the other difficulties and problems that face us? In the deanery in which I am currently working, only three of the twenty-one priests are below pension age. In this situation, it is fairly inevitable that there would be a lessening of energy and enthusiasm for the task. I have gone on record many times lamenting the lack of leadership coming from the Irish bishops. I have often noted that energy is more likely to be found among the ordinary Catholics than the ministers of the church. So I was very interested to read recently about a development in the church in the United States. I refer to gatherings called 'lay synods'. Lay Catholics are getting together to plan how to make the church more engaging and help it to live up to its potential. This movement began in a diocese in Illinois five years ago, and is now spreading across the country.

What is really interesting about these meetings, particularly in the American context, is that they are not protest meetings, not a group of liberal lay Catholics attacking the institutional church. As one of the organisers said: 'I've been at meetings in the past that were filled with vitriol and pessimism. The tone of the meetings was: "We're pissed off and we're not going to take it anymore".' This is a feature of Catholic life that America has experienced much more than we have here. There was a period of deep anger over the child abuse issue in the church that expressed itself through organisations like *Voice of the Faithful* and *Call to Action*. They adopted a position of intense criticism of church authorities, and organised such things as bans and boycotts in various parishes and dioceses. It is an interesting fact in itself that we haven't experienced anything similar within the church in Ireland over the past ten or fifteen years. Now it would appear there is a change of mood in America.

The anger is subsiding, and is being replaced by a more constructive attitude. These meetings are about 'conversation, reconciliation and respect'. A big effort is being made to draw in the different groups and mentalities within the church. This is very important. One of the major debilitating factors in the last thirty years or so has been the big split between the people of so-called 'liberal' and 'conservative' views. I have received far more vitriolic attacks and criticism from within the church than outside it over the years. It brings to mind the sentence in the gospels about how a house divided against itself cannot stand. These meetings are a real effort to bring an end to that division, and to mobilise all the different strands of church opinion to work together. So they have decided at these meetings not to deal with controversial issues like the ordination of women.

To give an example of how they go about it, one meeting in San Francisco recently had a very open-ended agenda. After two keynote addresses and a presentation by a Franciscan peace group about how to disagree respectfully, the gathering broke into small groups to discuss two questions: What good things are happening in your parishes that give you life? What are your 'desert experiences' in the church? The organisers said the first question was meant to generate a list of 'best practices', specific, practical examples that could be replicated in other parishes. The second question was meant to point to where change was necessary. Lastly, the groups were asked to suggest some strategies for 'moving from the desert to best practice'.

I think this is an excellent idea. I have always felt that the future of the church in Ireland depends on the lay people. Up to now little enough has come from them. We have groups like *We are Church* and *Pobal* trying to raise awareness and generate ideas, and they do good work. But they are small organisations with limited influence. I know also that some dioceses have made considerable efforts to involve the people in meetings, programmes and study courses. But they have come from the bishop and the priests. This movement in America seems more like something that could begin to mobilise and activate a much larger section of the Catholic faithful. It is coming from the people themselves. Maybe some Irish Catholics could take up the idea and begin to run with it.

A Quick Mass

Beauvoir sur Mer is a small town on the west coast of France. I was there on the morning of the 15th of August just as the church bell was ringing. I had been looking out for some place where I could go to Mass for the feast of the Assumption, so this was my chance. To my surprise, the church was full. Though there was probably a higher than the national average group of older people there, the congregation was quite representative of the ages and sexes. Just before the Mass was due to begin a woman came out and invited people to come over to a side chapel and take a candle for the entry procession. I did what any self-respecting Irish man would do in that situation. I sat tight, down near the back. But people went up easily, until the woman had got her quota. Then the entrance procession began, with the people carrying the candles, and another woman leading the singing. It was remarkable how well everyone sang. When the procession reached the altar the candles were placed so as to make the name MARIA. This set the tone both in terms of pace and involvement.

The priest was an old man, but he entered into the spirit of the event, and in no way did he inhibit the people around him. It was a lovely Mass, and even though I struggled with my poor French to understand what was being said some of the time, I felt totally at home in a warm, prayerful atmosphere. When it was over I looked at my watch and realised that it had lasted for one hour and five minutes. I was surprised, because it had seemed much shorter.

About ten days later, on my way to a match in Croke Park, I found myself at the ten o'clock Sunday Mass in a church in the south side of Dublin city, once again sitting down among the congregation. The crowd was small, a scattering of people in a large church. There was no singing, and a minimum of involvement of any sort. The sermon lasted for three minutes, and the whole Mass for thirty-two. But it seemed like an eternity. It was devoid of atmosphere, or any feeling of warmth or community. I did not experience it as being prayerful. But it was a quick Mass. It did me no good at all.

In the Irish church we have largely succumbed to the pressure to have short, quick Masses, with increasingly brief sermons. I have come to the conclusion that we have made a major mistake. The solution is not to be found in short Masses, but in good ones. Good Masses need time. Time to create atmosphere; time for people to be involved in as many and as creative ways as possible. Time for singing, and for getting the whole congregation singing. Time for silence. And time to create a sense of everything being unhurried, because we are glad to be here, and we know that it is the most important thing we will do in the day or the week. Where the priest is under pressure to get the Mass over quickly he will tend not to try anything new or different, or to invite people to be creative. He will fall back on doing it all himself. It is easier that way. He will do it quickly, conscious of the need to let the people go. So the underlying message will be of someone trying to get it over as fast as he can, someone who doesn't really regard this event as important. If it was the main event of his day, why rush so quickly to the end?

I know this is not a popular idea, and when I have mentioned it to some of my friends they have looked at me as if it was the final indication that I had gone totally mad, but my suggestion is that we should decide that every weekend Mass would last for one hour, with the possible exception of the early Sunday morning ones. Then let us face up to the challenge of how we can fill that hour in such a way that the people participating will feel that it only lasted for fifteen minutes, like I did at the Mass in France. It would force us priests to search our communities for the myriad of people with talent, and begin to give them their head. It would mean a lot of time and work. Maybe other things would have to give way. But surely there is nothing more important that we could spend our time at than preparing our Sunday Eucharist.

A Reflection on Celibacy

When I mentioned to a friend of mine, a woman in her fifties, that I had just come from a three day conference on sex, she asked me who was attending. I told her that there were about eighty of my confrères in the Redemptorists. Knowing that our average age is over sixty she started to laugh, and it took her some moments to contain herself. 'Isn't it late in your lives that you're discovering it', she said, 'but I suppose it's better late than never.' I tried to explain to her that sexual energy had to do with all forms of relationships in life, not just getting into bed with someone. But I could see her eyes begin to glaze over, and I changed the subject.

The conference was entitled 'Being Human, Sexual and Celibate', and it was conducted by an American woman, a nun and a psychologist. She was a bright, lively speaker, though she had an unfortunate habit of continuing without pause for anything up to an hour and three quarters, without any apparent diminution in her own energy. The same could not be said for us, her audience. But it was the first time in my experience that we, the Redemptorists, had gathered to listen to some straight talking on the subject, and to engage in an admittedly fairly limited amount of discussion. Like the dog walking on its hind legs, the wonder was that we did it at all.

It is now forty four years since I joined the Redemptorists and forty-three since I made my first commitment to live the celibate life. That was back in the early nineteen sixties. Coming from a small rural parish in County Galway, my upbringing was radically different to what it would be today. Education was scarce, and work more so. Being the youngest of a family of four, all of whom joined Religious life, it seemed only natural for me to follow suit. The influence of the nearby Redemptorist monastery was enormous on us. It was before the advent of free education and the school buses, so the boys in my family went to secondary school in the Redemptorist junior seminary in Limerick. I often ask myself why I stayed in Religious life and the priesthood. It is a hard question to answer. When one gets into a system it is sometimes easier to go along rather than to make the break. In the Catholic Church, celibacy is linked inextricably with priesthood, and my desire was to be a priest rather than a religious. The reason I choose the Redemptorists was partly due to their proximity, and also because the type of work they do suited my particular talents. Public speaking has always come easily to me, and I am seldom more alive than when I stand with a microphone in front of a large crowd of people.

The gospels tell us that consecrated celibacy is a gift from God, a charism given to some and not to most. For a long time now, I have believed that making celibacy mandatory for priesthood is wrong and oppressive. A charism, given as a free gift by God, is something that has to be accepted and lived out freely for its own sake, rather than making it a condition of another and quite separate form of life.

I have little or no doubt at this stage in my life that I was not a recipient of that charism, that gift from God that is consecrated celibacy. I also know that in this I am not unique, but that there are many priests of my generation who are in the same position. Was I aware of that in my mid twenties when I made my final profession and was ordained? I certainly was not. It is very difficult to look back almost forty years and accurately assess one's state of understanding at the time. I have managed to live it out in my own way, working out certain *modi vivendi* along the way. I have been lucky in the people I have known who have helped me. I am also lucky that my sexual energy did not emerge in an abusive fashion at any stage of my life. (I also suffered from sexual abuse as a young boy – I have written about this before – and our lecturer at the seminar told us that people like me run a higher risk of becoming abusers ourselves, or else being addicted to alcohol or cybersex; particularly if they have not gone for long periods of counselling to sort ourselves out, which I haven't!) I have loved the work I did as a priest, and continue to love it, even with a good bit less energy for the task than I had in my earlier years. In many ways it has been a good life, and I have no reason to complain about my lot, but if I was to have it all over again I think I might do it differently.

Celibacy as a consecrated way of life has been part of the church from the early centuries, but only became mandatory for all priests around the eleventh century. The theology that was used to justify and give value to the celibate life was fairly straightforward. It was quite simply considered a better and higher state of living. A celibate person lived a holier life than a married one, and consequently had a greater chance of eternal salvation. All sexual relationships were in some way sinful, even married ones. Sex was tolerated within marriage for the purposes of procreation, but every effort was made to limit its frequency, and to surround it with feelings of guilt. In the old duality of body and soul, sex was the most dominant of the bodily passions, and the more it could be controlled the better. It was considered best to live a life in which sex did not play any part.

The rules that underpinned celibate living were equally clear. The celibate priest should avoid contact with women as much as possible, and where it was absolutely necessary it must be kept to a minimum. There was no question of forming any sort of friendship with women; that would be regarded as an occasion of sin. Even friendship of what was known as a 'particular' kind with other males was forbidden. The celibate was told that his relationship was to be with Christ, and no other. Even his family must be kept at a distance.

That philosophy of celibate living worked well in the church for many centuries, in the sense that all priests in the Catholic Church had to remain celibate, and they were generally honoured and respected for doing so. This very respect increased the status of the priesthood, and was a major factor in the commonly accepted assumption that priests were holier than the rest of humanity. This is a very important point. In order to get people to accept a way of life that involves sacrifice and self-denial, it is a great help if it carries with it a degree of deference and status. The fact that living the celibate life is no longer regarded as admirable by people generally is a change of great significance.

Now the stricture remains the same, in that celibacy is still mandatory for the Catholic priesthood (with some exceptions which have been well publicised), but the rationale being presented for it, and the guidelines for how to live it out are radically different, and, in some instances, are the opposite of what they were. Our lecturer told us, contrary to what had been taught in the past, that intimacy was essential to the life of a celibate. She outlined in graphic detail the consequences for us if we fail to develop this intimacy. We will suffer from isolation, loneliness and stress, lack a healthy self-identity, be drawn towards compulsive, addictive lifestyles, and look for love and intimacy in all the wrong places. This sounds like a fairly dreadful state to be in. In olden days people were threatened with hell if they failed to live as they should. Now the threat is different – lives of unhappiness, addiction, God knows what. Which is the more fearful? I wondered as I listened if all those celibates who for centuries lived out their lives believing that intimacy was an occasion of sin, and a danger to their salvation had actually lived lives of quiet desperation. Somehow, I don't thinks so.

She went on to tell us that intimacy must be with women as well as men. There are twelve ways, she said, in which intimacy can be achieved. She listed them out for us: genital intimacy, emotional intimacy, intellectual intimacy, aesthetic intimacy, creative intimacy, recreational intimacy, work intimacy, crisis intimacy, conflict intimacy, commitment intimacy, spiritual intimacy and communication intimacy. Of those only one, the first, is forbidden for the celibate. 'Eleven out of twelve isn't bad!' she said and she bade us not to be greedy. I wasn't quite convinced.

But I could agree with a lot of what she said. Life has taught me the importance of trying to develop a connection with one or two people that is true and lasting. If, as a priest, you can have that sort of relationship with a woman without it becoming enormously complicated it is a great gift. It is very difficult, and many do not achieve it. But as I listened to her, my biggest question was this. Is it possible to take a lifestyle which has survived for centuries underpinned by a particular philosophy and way of living, and retain the lifestyle but turn the philosophy underpinning it on its head, and dramatically change the way it which it is to be lived out? I don't think so. While it sounded good coming from our speaker, I felt that it didn't fully hang together. You cannot change the whole way of thinking about something without undermining its very *raison d'être*. I am not suggesting that we go back to the old days of repression, even though it worked at a certain level.

But the new way of thinking does not fully connect with the reality of my experience. It is far too idealistic and demands a level of maturity and detachment that most people do not achieve until later in life, if at all. Whereas the celibate is supposed to put this into practice at a time in life when sexual energy is at its greatest, and personal maturity is often undeveloped and confused. In some way I think the old system, while repressive, was more in touch with the reality of human frailty.

Where does all this leave my view on celibacy? I acknowledge that the gift is given to some, and I am sure that such people are in some important way oriented towards living it out. I also know that celibacy lived truly for the sake of the kingdom is a good and wholesome thing. The only way to restore it to where it belongs is to remove it as a condition for any other form of life so that it stands on its own. It is then no longer necessary for priesthood, or maybe even for religious life, though that would involve a very imaginative rethinking of forms of religious life that might be adaptable to our modern world.

Our conference also dealt with the question of sexual orientation. This was in deference to the perception that both priesthood and religious life appear to have a higher proportion of people of a homosexual orientation than the ordinary population. Our lecturer informed us that the most commonly accepted view in the psychological community is that sexual orientation is not chosen, but discovered – in other words, one is born with it. She also said that a person's orientation is normal, even if it may not be seen by society as the norm.

This led to some interesting discussion, and considerable difference of opinion, particularly in relation to the moral consequences of what she was saying. People were asking how this fits in with the teaching of the church which says that homosexuality is a disorder. I was disappointed that the lecturer was not willing to follow through on the logic of her statement, and distance herself from the moral stance of the church. Instead she fudged and waffled, like a politician who did not want to give a hostage to fortune by answering a straight question. Though some of the men of homosexual orientation among us were clearly happy with her presentation, in that it gave them recognition and affirmation, I felt that what she said only scratched the surface of the difficult human and moral questions that sexual orientation raises for priesthood and Catholic Church morality.

So what do we know at the end of it all? Actually, I am not sure. Sexuality is profoundly personal and goes to the heart of who we are as human beings. It is a powerful force in our lives and, unless we can integrate into our humanity, it is capable of great destruction. Celibates need to integrate it as much as anyone else, and I presume that we all do it in our own individual ways. Sexuality is probably the area of life where Christ's words 'Judge not and you shall not be judged' most apply.

A Simple Blessing?

A priest is often asked to give a blessing. It is a relatively small and simple part of a priest's work. A short prayer, a sign of the cross and it is done. In the course of my priestly life I have blessed people in all sorts of situations and circumstances: I have blessed houses, animals, boats, endless religious objects, water and many, many other things. It is hard to imagine any situation in which you would refuse to give a blessing when it is genuinely requested. But there is one situation in which the church regularly refuses to give a blessing. It is the case of two people getting married who, for whatever reason, are not eligible for the official wedding ceremony of the church. Usually it is because one of both of them has been married before. When a couple in this situation come to a priest asking for a blessing, they are usually refused.

John and Mary (I am using the names that were standard in the old Redemptorist mission sermon on company-keeping, which outlined in graphic detail the road to perdition that this young couple were on!) were getting married recently. Mary, in her late thirties, was getting married for the first time. John, around fifty, had been married before. His first marriage had broken up early; after some years of separation they tried again, but now it was finally ended and he was divorced. Mary is quite a religious person, who goes to Mass every Sunday and is involved with her local church. John also goes to Mass, though not every weekend. They understood completely that they could not have a wedding ceremony in the church, and that what they were doing was not in accordance with church teaching. They had no argument with that. But equally they believed that the love they had for each other was real and true, and they were anxious to have some form of blessing on their life together and on their commitment. They approached Mary's local priest, whom she knew well and who was a family friend. They enquired about the possibility of having a quiet ceremony, either in the church or in their home, in which he would simply ask God to bless them and their life together. The poor man was clearly embarrassed. He wished them well, and was very well disposed towards them, but said that unfortunately he could do nothing for them. Because they are a mature and considerate couple, they understood his dilemma and it did not end the friendship. They next went to a neighbouring priest, who was friendly with John. Again he received them kindly, and wished them well. But he said that, in view of the position adopted by their own priest, he could not offer them any sort of blessing. Again they parted on very good terms, the couple saying that they understood his position. And yet, with all the good will in the world, it is unavoidable that a couple will see this as a rejection, even a condemnation of them.

Both priests were acting in accordance with the official position of the Catholic Church in this matter. Priests are strictly forbidden to give any form of recognition to a couple who are getting married outside of the narrow requirements of the church. The logic of this is that any form of blessing given to such a couple will be confused with the sacrament, and will serve to debase and devalue the church teaching on the sacredness of marriage. From a legal point of view this has a certain logic, but I'm afraid that pastorally it is cruel and unnecessary.

We are living in a complex and difficult society now. Marriages are breaking down. Considering the high pressure lives that young couples have to live today, I constantly marvel at how many are succeeding in holding a marriage together. The way that society is structured, the enormous price of houses, the difficulty of commuting to work, and may other things about life in modern Ireland, are inimical to sustaining long-term relationships. Can we in the church not find some way of supporting people who fail in their marriage, rather than passing a severe judgement on them, even to the extent of refusing a blessing? On the face of it, refusing to bless somebody who asks for a blessing is an extraordinarily judgemental thing to do. If the church is to be relevant in these times it has to turn its back on rigidity and develop a degree of flexibility to enable it to respond to the situations we are constantly meeting. Refusing people who come to us for some form of spiritual nourishment is a hopeless response. Can the Irish bishops do something about this?

A Woman in the Pulpit

A recent mission, in the parish of Ennis in County Clare, was interesting from a number of points of view. For many years now Ennis parish has committed itself to the principles of Vatican II, particularly in regard to the emphasis on community, on a real partnership between clergy, religious and laity, and on a high level of involvement in liturgical celebrations. The Irish church in general has given a great deal of lip service to these ideas, but in my experience any efforts at putting them into practice have been slow and tentative. From what I have seen around the country in my mission work, I would find it hard to think of any parish that is as alive and vibrant as Ennis. I like going there because I find it reassuring and affirming to see that the Vatican II notion of parish life does actually work when it is implemented with conviction and energy. And where it works, it is good to behold.

The second interesting aspect of our mission was the composition of the team that conducted the week. For most of my years as a missioner, I have worked with women as members of the team. But almost invariably they were young and very talented in music and singing, and even though they would occasionally talk, their main contribution was in the areas of music, singing, drama and working with youth. Being totally challenged as regards music and singing myself, I tended to automatically see the woman's role on the team as supplying what I lacked. Preaching was my area, and let them look after the rest. On this occasion we had a woman theologian, Fainche Ryan, with us. So she came in a different capacity, as one who would preach and speak to the people just as we, the clerical members of the team, were doing.

The first thing that became quickly evident was that the people seemed to make no distinction between her and the priests on the team. She seemed to be immediately and totally accepted, and I am not aware of anyone questioning her right to be there. I think one person raised the issue of whether she should be allowed to read the gospel at Mass, but that was all. Secondly, what she had to say was not regarded in any way as of lesser importance because she was not ordained. In fact the opposite gradually happened. As the week

34

went on she began to be seen as the person among us all who spoke with the most authority. This had something to do with the fact that we presented her as a theologian (that word needed to be explained for a lot of people!) who lectured in Cambridge, but I think it had also to do with the freshness of the feminine voice and perspective on the great Christian concerns. Having the thoroughness of the theologian, I saw her preparing her talks by consulting the *Documents of Vatican II* and the *Catechism of the Catholic Church*, neither of which the average Redemptorist missioner would be consulting in the hours before his mission sermons, since he would invariably have a lot of material in his bag from previous missions that he could call on. On the night we commemorated our dead, she gave about seven minutes on the Christian teaching on eternity, and to me, who had heard countless talks on the topic, it sounded fresh and new. To be fair, we were chided by one or two people afterwards because we had decided that on a night when we remembered and prayed for our dead we would not focus on hell. One man told me the next morning that we were too soft. Somehow, I took it as a compliment!

I came away from the week with a renewed conviction of how we in the Catholic Church are so impoverishing our preaching by restricting it to men, and clergy at that. Having worked along with Fainche, and shared the pulpit with her for the week, I cannot accept a thesis that would suggest that the Spirit of God was speaking more powerfully through me or my fellow priests than through her.

Now in my sixties, the more energetic part of my life as a preacher of the Christian message is definitely behind me and my contemporaries who were the last of the large numbers of vocations. There are few enough young priests coming up behind to take our place. Who is going to preach the message to future generations? There are people willing and able to do so. If the faith is not passed on because of the rigidity of the church's stance on who is entitled to preach, then maybe it will deserve what it gets! But not the people whose lives will be impoverished because they have not heard the Word of Life.

An Apology

I was wandering around a country graveyard on a lovely spring evening when a friend called me over. She pointed to a headstone. 'Look at that one,' she said. Headstones are usually not very informative and this was no different. The person had died about twenty-five years previously at the age of eighty, had been a teacher, and an unmarried woman. That was all.

'She taught me,' my friend said, 'She came to our school back in the nineteen fifties when the number of pupils increased. She was a third teacher in the school, but there were only two classrooms, so a curtain was hung across the Master's room, and in that confined area she taught second, third and fourth class. She was not a good teacher, possibly with little or no qualifications, and she could be cruel and harsh at times.'

My friend settled into her story, telling me how she could remember a day when she was in fifth class, sitting with another girl in a desk at the back of the Master's classroom, right next to the curtain. The priest was visiting, and he and the master were deep in conversation at the window, so the class took the opportunity to chat with each other, and as long as they didn't make too much noise, the master didn't mind.

'Gradually, we became aware of a commotion on the other side of the curtain. The teacher was beating a boy for not knowing his lesson, and he was crying loudly. We knew who it was and, as we would say nowadays, he suffered from a learning disability. We described it differently in those days. We were upset at the way the teacher was treating him. I turned to the curtain and said: "Aw, miss, stop hitting him!" I didn't mean her to hear, but I must have spoken more loudly than I intended. The curtain opened, she stormed through and up to the master and the priest. The investigation quickly revealed myself as the culprit, and the master put me kneeling behind his desk for the rest of the day. Before going home he told me to write out an apology to the teacher and bring it in next day. My big worry was that my parents would hear of it, since in those days parents tended to back up the teacher, and I suspected I might be more severely punished by them.'

'What was in your apology?' I asked, absorbed in her story, and looking down at the grave.

'It was short and to the point. "Dear Miss, I am sorry for saying what I said yesterday." I signed it, and next morning I left it on the master's desk. Happily, that brought the matter to a close without my parents learning of it, and I could relax again. But there is a sequel to the story, and you've got to remember when it happened. It was the Ireland of the nineteen fifties; this woman was about sixty years of age, and I was ten. A few days after the incident in the school, my mother sent me to the local shop for some messages. The shop owner was a relation of the teacher, and when I walked in I was taken aback to find the teacher herself behind the counter. Acting as normally as I could, I asked for my messages and then handed over the money. As she gave me the change, the teacher spoke: 'Mary,' she said, 'I want to apologise to you for the other day. I am sorry I made such a fuss.' I was amazed. In those days an adult did not apologise to a child. I thanked her and went out.'

We both stood at the grave in silence for a moment, thinking of the old teacher whose bones lay in the ground beneath us.

'You know,' my friend said, 'If it hadn't been for that apology, I wouldn't even stand at this grave. I would remember her, if I remembered her at all, as a hard, cruel old woman. But now I think of that lovely moment of humanity, when an old teacher apologised to a little girl. Because of that moment I can think of her with affection, and I am happy to pray that she is at peace.'

Assisting Death

'You can do anything in Ireland as long as you don't talk about it.' I thought of that comment from a friend when the issue of mercy killing, or euthanasia, raised its head recently. Some leading members of the Church of Ireland suggested that it was a topic that we as a society could usefully discuss. My initial reaction to their position was that it represented the thin end of the wedge. Once we began to discuss mercy killing we would inevitably be opening the door that would eventually allow it to happen. That was until a nurse introduced me to the uses and possible abuses of the syringe driver. I know that for many years in Irish hospitals and hospices some patients, especially those who are in pain or distress, are given increasing doses of morphine in their last days. The morphine helps to dull the pain, to quieten the distress, but it also hastens the end. Putting up the syringe driver is the medical term used for administering the morphine. Can this be called mercy killing? Is it euthanasia? I suspect that in some cases it is.

I understand that this form of intervention is justified by the medical profession in the interests of alleviating pain. Hastening the death of the patient is a possible but not directly intended side-effect. As such one can argue that it is not euthanasia, because the intention is not to kill the patient but to lessen the pain. I am not totally convinced. At the very least it is a practice that is open to abuse.

An old woman was dying in hospital. She clearly hadn't a lot of time left. She might die in a few days, or she might linger on for some weeks or even months. When a person is dying from the general symptoms of old age it is often difficult, even for the most skilled medical practitioner, to accurately forecast the time of death. This woman was distressed. The distress was not caused so much by pain as by unhappiness. Death is the biggest adventure and probably the greatest challenge that every human person has to meet. We have to go there alone. No matter how often we have witnessed the death of others, we go into the mystery of our own death without any roadmap. The advent of death forces us to look back on our lives, and come face to face with any unfinished business.

There were unresolved issues in this woman's life, and now they were coming starkly before her. Because of her advanced years she sometimes lost her grip of present reality and drifted back into the past. But the lucid moments were the unhappy ones. She told a nurse that she was unhappy, and the chaplain came. Unfortunately he was too focused on doing his sacramental duty, and failed to give her time and space to talk. She was still unhappy when he left. She tossed about in the hospital bed, restless and anxious. The nurses were, as always, under pressure. They found it hard to watch the poor woman in such distress. After a brief consultation with the doctor they put up the syringe driver. The woman gradually lost touch with reality. Any chance she had to work out the issues that needed to be worked out in order for her to die in peace was now gone. As her distress continued the dose of morphine was increased. Two days later the woman was dead. Despite the morphine her death was not easy.

Was that a compassionate use of the syringe driver? Was it an act of kindness to give that woman morphine? I don't think so. Whose needs were being met in administering the medicine? Probably those of the carers rather than the patient. Real kindness would have involved trying to keep her lucid for as long as possible, even if that involved enduring some pain, and providing her with the best possible help to come to terms with her approaching death and to find peace.

A great deal depends on a person's belief. If I as a medical person do not believe in a life after death, then it will make perfect sense for me to alleviate any form of distress, be it physical, psychological or emotional, in the patient's last days. But if both I and the patient believe in an eternal life, I will have a different perspective. I will want that person to enter the next life with as little baggage and as much peace as possible. I will be more cautious and reluctant in my use of the syringe driver. I will know that sometimes it is only by facing the causes of distress and taking the necessary action that a person can find peace. Showing compassion to the patient could mean very different things, depending on my own belief and that of the patient.

The Church of Ireland spokespeople were probably right. We as a society do need to discuss the issue of euthanasia. It would appear that the thin end of the wedge is already very much in place.

Baptising a Child

The young woman looked about fourteen, but she was in fact in her early twenties. Her aunt, who brought me to meet her, told me that though she was unmarried she was doing a very good job as mother to her three month old daughter. She didn't attend church and she had asked her aunt to organise the baptism of the child. I was to be officiating at the ceremony on the following Sunday. She was no longer dating the father, but he was involved with the child, and they were getting on well.

When we arrived at the meeting place she was waiting, but the father had not yet arrived. After the usual niceties her aunt began to ask her some questions. She was more direct and straight with her questions than I would have dared to be. 'You don't go to Mass yourself; why do you want to have your child baptised?' I could see there was a fair degree of ease between aunt and niece, but still the young woman was baffled by the question. After a few moments of thought she responded. 'I want to give her a start, and then she can make up her own mind when she grows up.' I am familiar with that argument being used in exactly the opposite way, as a justification for not giving any religious training to a child, but I kept silent

'Does God mean anything to you?' This question was beyond her, she had no idea how to deal with it. She expressed her bafflement, so her aunt rephrased the question: 'Do you ever pray?' 'I did when I was having my child?' 'Were you afraid?' I asked. 'Terrified', she answered. 'And when it was all over did you thank God?' her aunt asked. 'I do that every day when I look at what a perfect child I have'. There was some religious sensibility there, even if there was no contact with the church.

I said that at the ceremony she would make a commitment to train her child in the ways of the faith, to bring her up as a practising Catholic. 'Will you bring her to Mass?' her aunt asked. She laughed off the question in an embarrassed way, and it was not pursued.

At this point the father of the child, who happened to be minding the little girl for the weekend, arrived with the baby. She was indeed a perfect little child. He was about the same age as the mother, tall and thin, and wearing the jersey of his county team.

After the introductions, and the usual cooing over the baby, the aunt began to ask him some of the same questions, though a bit more cautiously, since there wasn't a blood relationship to bridge the gap between them. He was more embarrassed, and seemed to experience greater difficulty in trying to answer them. He did tell us that while he grew up in a home where at least one of his parents went to Mass, he had stopped going himself when he left primary school. Questions about what God meant to him, whether he prayed, and why he wanted his daughter baptised seemed to be new to him, the sort of issues he hadn't given any serious thought to.

At this point the baby began to cry, which drew the attention of mother and aunt. I took the opportunity to chat with him, and, conscious of the county jersey, I began to talk about hurling. He immediately relaxed, and had plenty to say. He suggested what was wrong with his own county team, and wasn't short on opinions about the problems of my native county, Galway.

There was never any question that we would not baptise the child. The network of friendships involved would have made that decision difficult. Both parents were sure that they wished her to receive the sacrament, and anyway they were such lovely young people, and they both clearly loved the child, so I would not have felt comfortable refusing them. The invitations were already gone out, and the place for the get-together was booked. When I spoke a bit about the sacrament, and the various parts of the ceremony, they began to show real interest at the idea of the anointing with the oil of exorcism. I said it was to protect the child against all the evil that might beset her in life. All four of us looked over at the tiny little girl in the carry cot, and it was obvious that she would need all the help she could get in this difficult world. That meant much more to them than any notion about becoming part of the community of believers, of which they themselves were not members.

I could see the dilemma that must face priests who work in parishes on a regular basis. These two young parents are no different to many parents who do not attend Mass but still want their children to be baptised, receive First Communion and Confirmation.

Indeed, one could say that these two at least had the question of religious belief and practice posed to them. The church needs to face up to this issue through some type of adult instruction. Some people criticise the standard of religious education in the schools. They say that the young generation have no grounding in the faith, that they are largely ignorant of what it teaches. That may well be true, but I suspect that the problem is deeper.

I recently heard Michael D. Higgins calling for the introduction of philosophy into the secondary school curriculum. I thought of that as we talked to the young couple. I know religious knowledge is important, but I think that even more important is the ability to face the big philosophical questions about life and its meaning that are the basis of all religious belief. Our generation was introduced to those questions through the classical content of our education. In today's system it is missing.

Different Ways to Interpret Laws

'For one of them law is a means of control, and for the other it is a way to liberation.' So said a Redemptorist confrère of mine one morning at breakfast, describing two priests who had studied canon law in the Philippine Islands. He marvelled at how both of them has done the same courses of study, but had come out with radically opposite attitudes to the subject.

But of course it is true that different people and different nationalities view the law and its application in very different ways. As I write this article there is a developing controversy about a Vatican document which is expected to say that men of a homosexual orientation will no longer be allowed into seminaries to study for the priesthood. It is believed by many, especially in the Western world, that there is a higher than average number of gays entering seminaries today. And now the Vatican are determined to act, and put an end to this. Or so I thought, and I expected that this would cause considerable debate.

So I went on the internet to see what John Allen had to say on the topic. John L. Allen is the Vatican correspondent for the *National Catholic Reporter*, an American newspaper that covers religious issues. He has been a long time in Rome, and he knows the people and the *modus operandi* of the Vatican very well. He posts an article on the internet each week under the title *A Word from Rome*, and it often makes for interesting reading. What he had to say about this document was particularly thought-provoking, since he went into the whole question of law and the different ways that people view its application in their lives. His very first sentence had me sitting up:

> The forthcoming Vatican document on gays in seminaries will unleash a wrenching debate about Catholicism and homosexuality, but one thing it certainly will not mean is that in the future there will be no gays in the priesthood.

Since it seemed to me that any logical interpretation of the document would suggest that blocking gays from priesthood is exactly what it is intended to do, I wondered what he could mean. I read on.

> 'Although it is a difficult point for many Anglo-Saxons to grasp, when the Vatican makes statements like "no gays in the priesthood" it doesn't actually mean "no gays in the priesthood". Instead, it means, "As a general rule this is not a good idea, but we all know there will be exceptions".'

Allen goes on to explain that in order to understand this distinction we need to appreciate the Italian concept of law, which holds sway in the Vatican. Law, according to them, expresses an ideal. It describes a perfect state of affairs from which many people, indeed everybody to a greater or lesser extent, will inevitably fall short. Allen quotes a Vatican official: 'Law describes the way things would work if people were angels.' And since none of us are angels, they don't really expect their laws to be closely observed.

This is a very different way of looking at law to what is commonly understood in America, Britain, and to a slightly lesser extent here in Ireland. We are inclined to expect law to dictate what people actually do, rather than just the ideal. This is an important point, which is behind a lot of the confusion that can arise in the church over laws and regulations. In the Anglo-Saxon world the Italian approach to law can be seen as a form of hypocrisy, the church issuing laws and turning a blind eye to the people who disobey them. But Vatican officials view it instead as a realistic concession to fallen human nature. These two different understandings of law were very much at the heart of the whole debate over *Humanae Vitae*, the papal document on contraception some years ago. Here in Ireland, the church was trying to get people to accept it literally, and put it into practice in their lives. The Italians, on the contrary, looked on it as the ideal, and did not really expect people to live up to it. So, while we were telling people in confession that using contraceptives was seriously sinful, they had a much more relaxed attitude to it. Theologians and bishops' conferences in Northern Europe at the time were trying to find formulas to allow people some flexibility in their personal lives. The Vatican resisted these interpretations of the document, because they wanted to preserve the statement of ideal in all its purity. They did not feel the need to give people flexibility, because they knew that the Italian mentality would automatically understand it as an ideal statement rather than a rigid law. Unfortunately, many ordinary Catholics, unaware of the different understanding of law at work in the argument, had great difficulty working it out in their own lives.

Believers are in the Minority

I am surprised at how much of a struggle I am having within myself in coming to terms with the rapid decline in faith and church attendance in modern Ireland. I am under the impression that, for whatever reason, the past year has seen an acceleration in that trend, to the extent that it has now become a flowing tide. It affects me in my work, the preaching of missions and novenas. I find myself still asking priests, when I go to a parish to prepare for a mission, what is the population of the parish. And then I estimate from that what the likely response will be. When I find, as I increasingly do, that the response is less than I expected, I am disappointed. I make the mistake of focusing on all the people who are not coming to the mission, and it can sometimes be a struggle to sustain the enthusiasm and energy for the work. Of course, the priests of the parish are often afflicted with the same type of thinking. 'I looked at the crowd tonight,' one local priest said to me after a mission night that I felt was well attended, 'and I thought of whole areas of the parish that were not represented.' We are so trained to think in terms of everybody coming that when we look at a crowd we are inclined to see those who are not there rather than those who are.

I like to do a youth night on a mission, a night when the young people of the parish are involved in the presentation of the service. When it works well it is great, and generally tends to be the night that creates most excitement in the week. But it is getting harder to gather a sufficient group of young people who are willing to come forward and volunteer their time and energy to making it a success. Recently, in a parish where I failed to get the young people involved, the local catechist in the secondary school told me bluntly that when she spoke to them about it they just were not interested. 'There are only three of the fifth years going to Mass, and it is too hard for them to stand out from the others who regard the whole thing as for the birds!'

The reality of Ireland today is that those who are in any serious manner attempting to follow the Christian way of life are in a minority. This is true not only in the big cities, but also in the small towns and now in the country parishes as well. It would greatly help priests like me, and even more so those who work in parishes, to try to fully accept that reality. I know it in my head. I have often talked and preached about it, saying that this day would come. But at an emotional level I am finding it hard to face. I still want to gather all the people of the parish, and I want to bring back those who have given up the practice of their faith. I have been inclined to think that they have drifted away, somewhat by accident or maybe through laziness, and that if they could be started up again everything would be grand. I need to tell myself that, in most instances, this is no longer the case. They have actually made a choice. Modern Irish society is living by values that are very different to those of the gospel. Materialism has become the dominant philosophy. What this essentially means is that people have made the acquiring of material wealth and possessions the greatest priority of their existence. This is the antithesis of the teaching of Christ. More and more people are choosing this way of life. Many of our young people are choosing a life that involves the consumption of drugs and alcohol, often in large quantities in order to achieve a state of oblivion, and sexual freedom without responsibility. These too are contrary to the Christian way. I am increasingly reminded of Moses coming down the mountain and finding his people worshipping the golden calf. It seems to me that the majority of people in Ireland today have set up their golden calf, and have turned their backs on the God of their ancestors.

The implications of this for how the church has traditionally organised itself are enormous. Is it time we forgot about the notion that everyone who lives within the confines of the parish, and who does not belong to another church, is a Catholic? Do we need instead to have a membership ceremony for those who wish to belong, and that would involve a commitment to attend church regularly? In this case would we no longer provide services like first communions, weddings, funerals for those who do not belong? This would be a highly controversial and divisive thing to do. *Liveline* would get numerous programmes out of people airing their grievance about the uncaring church who was turning them, or worse still, their children, away! But maybe in the end it would be a more honest and truthful situation for all concerned.

Blind Patriotism

*(This article was written while on a mission in Atlanta
just before the war in Iraq. It is interesting in hindsight.)*

As I write this it is the end of January, and I am conducting a mission in a parish in Atlanta, Georgia. This is one of the southern states, in what is known as the Bible belt. As I walk two miles each day along Peachtree Road I pass five Christian churches, the Catholic Church in which I am working, the Dunwoody Methodist Church, Episcopalian and Anglican Churches in close proximity, and, down at the end of the street where Peachtree meets the Interstate Highway, the First Baptist Church of Atlanta. This one, a converted warehouse with a capacity of two and a half thousand, is reputed to be the biggest church in the city. Of course I'm in Baptist country. They have the allegiance of the large majority of believers in these parts. But all the churches are clearly going concerns. These are church-going people.

The parish I am in is also holding its end up. Sunday Masses are well attended. There is a large staff of lay people working for the church. The collection each weekend is bigger than many an Irish parish would get in a whole year. The people are friendly and enthusiastic, and their devotion to the church is obvious. The man who picked me up at the airport, a member of the Knights of Columbus, wore a badge that proclaimed, 'We support our priests.'

A fever of patriotism has gripped the nation, or at least this part of it, which makes it, from my perspective, rather frightening. The people don't want to discuss the possibility of war with Iraq, except to assure me that, just as they support the priests, they also support the president. They tell me Mr Bush is a supporter of life. When I injudiciously mentioned Bill Clinton at dinner one evening, the monsignor, an Irish American in his late seventies, proclaimed loudly: 'He's a philanderer!' and that ended that line of conversation.

Mr Bush gave his State of the Union address two nights ago. The war and the economy were the two main topics. It was pointed out to me, with considerable approval, that he has invoked God in five of his last eight sentences. The fact that all those sentences were proposing an imminent attack on Iraq did not seem to contain any contradiction for those who spoke to me. But there was a letter in

the local paper this morning noting that when people are proposing war they tend to call on God, rather than on Jesus. It would not
be easy, the letter said, to sound convincing while invoking the person of Jesus ('Blessed are the peacemakers') in favour of war.

In my preaching I studiously avoided any mention of the possible war. I didn't know what to say, and I had no confidence that my
views on the subject would be well received. But I felt decidedly
uncomfortable, and somehow failing to preach the message. Paul
says that we should preach 'in season and out of season'. And Jesus
himself clearly didn't allow the prejudices of his audience to influence or weaken what he wanted to say. Of course he paid a high
price for his outspokenness.

It is interesting to see how a society, which is basically made up
of decent, good-living people, who are also quite religious, can be
so unquestioningly supportive of a conflict that may well mean the
death of many thousands of innocent people. (I am aware that in
other parts of the United States many are seriously questioning
what is proposed.) In the context of a highly emotional patriotism,
the sort induced by the events of September 11, the rhetoric of war
quickly turns the perceived enemy into non-people, and the conflict becomes a simple matter of good against evil, 'the axis of evil',
in the words of Mr Bush. The people stop listening to anything
that might give an alternative point of view. Something similar
must have happened to many good people in Germany who were
carried along in the wave of support for Hitler. I know it is
Saddham Hussein who has most in common with Hitler. But there
is something about blind patriotism that diminishes us as people.

By the time you, gentle reader (to quote Hugh Leonard!), read
this article, a lot might have happened. Maybe Mr Bush and the
Americans will have been proved correct, and the world will be rid
of a terrible tyrant. Maybe, on the other hand, unforeseen and cata-
strophic consequences will have followed an attack on Iraq, and
countless lives will be lost. Whatever the future holds, I will return
to Ireland in a day or two, relieved to be away from the 'patriot
game', from a mentality that sees God as backing one nation
against another. It's just a pity that I took the easy, and cowardly,
option in the preaching of my mission.

Britney Spears and Child Abuse

I sometimes think that if the people who phone Joe Duffy's *Liveline* on RTÉ Radio One are an accurate representation of the nation, we are in serious trouble. But listening to radio programmes in the US clearly establishes the fact that we are not the only country with people of extreme views who love to go on air. Maybe every society has a small group of people, not gifted with much common sense, who spend their time phoning in to talk-shows on the various radio programmes, and unburdening themselves of views that are unrepresentative, while the large majority of the people, if they listen to these shows, just shake their heads in disbelief and get on with living their lives.

Some years ago *Liveline* devoted a couple of programmes to the fact that Darina Allen, wife of Tim Allen, had returned to RTÉ television with a cookery programme. People who phoned in were outraged. 'How dare she show her face, considering what her husband had been sentenced for?' The fact that she herself was completely blameless of the behaviour in question didn't seem to make any difference to them. The outbreak of moral righteousness was loud and strident. There is something particularly unpleasant about moral righteousness delivered in a high-pitched tone.

What most irritated me about this rush to judgement was that it coincided with the Britney Spears concerts at the Point. Here was an event that was quite extraordinary. A pop star, who appeals to pre-pubescent girls, putting on a show that was explicitly sexual, even pornographic in parts. And thousands of young girls were brought to this concert by their parents. What could these parents possibly have been thinking about? They cannot claim that they did not know the nature of the event they were going to. Britney Spears has been on the go for a considerable time, and the style and content of her show was familiar. Anyone in any doubt would only have to switch to MTV on their television. By bringing their daughters to the concert the parents were clearly showing that they approved of this style of dress and behaviour. Is this really what they want their daughters to be learning at this very early age? Do they regard it as healthy and good for them? Or, worse still, are today's parents so incapable of refusing their children that they simply gave in to them?

What Tim Allen was accused of, downloading child pornography on the internet, is undoubtedly an abuse of children. It is a criminal activity, and he deserved to be punished. However, it should not in any way reflect on his wife, or on her profession. But I think that the show put on by Britney Spears is just as surely an abuse of children, introducing them to an explicit presentation of adult sexual activity, some of it perverse, in the context of music that appeals to them. I would even go so far as to suggest that the parent who brought her or his young daughter to the show could also be said to be guilty of child abuse. What else could exposing a ten-year-old girl to that show be called?

We are full of confusion and double standards in our attitude to sexuality. We are vehement in our condemnation of abusers, while we allow our children to be sexualised at an inappropriately young age. I think we have been influenced in this by the double standard and hypocrisy of the tabloid newspapers, who rail against some form of sexual deviation on page one while they show pictures of naked women in provocative poses on page three. *Prime Time* did have part of a programme on the Spears concert and raised questions about the appropriateness of exposing children to such images. However, as I watched that programme, I could not help noticing that it lacked the tone of moral outrage that it usually reserves for matters relating to the sexual abuse of children.

The other interesting feature of all of this is the silence of the church. I know that in the past the church had more than enough to say on sexual matters, and for various reasons has lost some of its credibility. But do we have to be totally silent? Why didn't some church person stand up and ask why thousands of parents were bringing their children to see Britney Spears? Why didn't I do it myself? We are all terrified of being branded as moralisers. But somebody in this country needs to get courage. Any society needs moral guardians, people who are capable of giving wisdom and guidance to us all. Children need role models, not ones who will corrupt and debase them, but ones who will show them the values necessary for a happy and healthy life.

Death and the Afterlife

What can we say about death and the afterlife? I think we do well on the ritual, but we have a problem with our efforts to explain what might be going on, to shed light on the mystery.

A young woman who had many questions recently visited me. Her brother, a man of about twenty-two, has died in a tragic accident a few months previously. She was clearly an intelligent person, but had only a basic education, and possessed a somewhat literal mind. She wanted answers, and I could see that it wasn't going to be easy to satisfy her. My carefully thought out theological concepts were not going to be of any use. She neither understood, nor was she interested in them.

Her first question was straight to the point. Could she be certain that her brother was in heaven? My effort at an answer talked about the goodness and love of God, and how he wants all people to be saved. But, she wanted to know, why didn't he come back and tell them? After all, she had loved him, and his young wife had loved him. If he really cared for them, and if he was now in the presence of God, why didn't he give them some sign? It would be a small thing to do, and it would make all the difference. But nobody has come back from the dead, I told her. What about Jesus? Didn't he come back, and if he did, why couldn't her brother do the same? She wasn't looking for a resurrection, just a sign that everything was all right.

That set her mind on another line of thought. If, as I was assuring her, I believed that he was with God, could he be happy there? Would it even be right for him to be happy? After all, he had left his young wife alone and widowed, with a broken heart. If his love for her was genuine, should he not also be suffering? Should he not be missing her desperately, and wanting to be with her? Though she wanted him to be there, still the thought of him up in heaven in complete contentment didn't seem quite right to her. You can't just leave behind a person you loved deeply, and be fully happy in your new state. There clearly was a certain logic to what she was saying, but while I searched for some useful response her mind had moved on.

The idea of purgatory; could it be possible that her brother was there? I said that maybe he was, I didn't know. But was that a punishment, and would he be suffering there? She had great difficulty with the notion of him being punished. He was a good man, she told me. He could quarrel and fight, but he had never left another person in intensive care. He was generous. The idea of a God who might want to punish him was beyond her understanding. I talked about purgatory as a process of development and maturing which made us ready for full life and love with God. She nodded her head, but I had no confidence that I was making sense for her. It all seemed so vague compared to the sharp clarity of her questions. How long would it last, she wanted to know, and should she pray for him? She was comfortable with the idea of prayer to shorten his stay in purgatory. It gave her something to do that she believed was helpful, and she clearly needed that. When I said that we could not speak of time in relation to the next life, that time was of this world only, she didn't really want to hear, because what was the point of praying if it didn't shorten the time he had to do.

She informed me she had visited a number of spiritual people, healers and the like. They had told her that her brother's destiny had been laid out for him. From the time he was born, the day and the nature of his death had all been decided. This was the plan of God. She said that one of them even told her that if he had avoided that particular death, he would probably have died a week or so later in a much more horrible way. I think she liked that idea. It seemed to provide an explanation, some way to make sense of it. At least she now knew who was responsible. She asked what I thought. I told her I had difficulty with the notion that it is all decided in advance. I believed that we had some say in our lives, and without that free will would be gone. I could see that the idea of free will was not as important to her as to me. She preferred answers.

When I heard the Dean of Clonmacnoise suggesting that we have a serious problem today with religious language and concepts, I could see something of what he meant.

Future of the Priesthood

I was glad to read that Dr Freeman, the new bishop of Ossory, in an interview with *The Irish Catholic*, suggested that importing foreign priests would not be the answer to the current problems of ministry in the Irish church. I fully agree with him. The places where priests are plentiful at the moment, like Nigeria, Poland and parts of the Far East, have a very different culture and understanding of church to us, so I don't see them fitting easily into the Irish situation. There would be a real danger that all the effort put into involving the laity in the running of parishes that has happened in recent years would be reversed, and we would return to the more clerical style of church of the middle of the last century. The bishop went on to say that it was the duty of a Christian community to nourish its own priestly vocations, and that he would initiate a new drive for vocations in his diocese. I wish him well, though I wouldn't have any great confidence that he will be successful.

I recently sat in on a conversation with a group of about thirty people, married and single, at which the discussion, among other things, concerned how we might find a solution to the rapid decline of clergy numbers and the problem this creates for ministry in the Irish church. Getting straight to what I regarded as one of the central questions, I asked them how they would feel about their own son becoming a priest. Their response showed a decided lack of enthusiasm, even though as a group they were committed to the church and the faith more than the average. To some extent the scandals are the elephant in the Irish church's kitchen at the moment, and while this group did not mention them at any stage in the discussion, it was hard to say how much their attitudes were influenced by them. In any case, I could see clearly that they did not consider the priesthood as a good career choice. They mentioned a number of issues.

Today's young generation do not look favourably on a profession that demands a life-long commitment. They prefer to be open to change, and work at a number of different professions in the course of life. I could sense in myself a negative reaction to this, thinking it was a sign of the lack of endurance of the young, but I wisely kept my mouth shut. The group seemed to look on it differently. If the church wanted to be relevant to the modern world it needed to be able to adapt to the times, rather than cling on to traditional ways of doing things. In other words, the possibility of engaging in ministry as a priest should be open to people for a set period of time rather than as a permanent commitment. That raises a very interesting question. Should the church adapt to the particular culture and attitudes of the age, or should it hold on rigidly to its traditional ways of doing things?

The majority of the group clearly were not fans of life-long celibacy, particularly of the compulsory variety. Rather than see celibacy as an admirable thing, much as it was seen in the past, they regarded it with a certain degree of scepticism, not at all sure that it was a psychologically healthy way of life, and maybe even with some suspicion. They could not see how being married would be a hindrance to effective ministry, but rather a help.

Among the group there were some with more radical views. Some of the women felt that the exclusion of women from priesthood was intolerable. They welcomed the decline in vocations to this particular form of priesthood as a good thing, probably the work of the Holy Spirit. They looked forward to the day when an exclusively male form of ministry died out, to be replaced by something very different. So they would not be promoting vocations under the present system. Neither would they pray for new candidates to join, but see empty seminaries as a sign of hope. This was the only way they felt that change would come. When the church had its back to the wall it would be forced to look more realistically at the situation. If the diocese of Ossory has many who think like this, it will certainly make Bishop Freeman's task more difficult.

The group liked Bishop Freeman's notion of the Christian community nourishing its own vocations, but they thought that would not be possible to do until such time as the church removed the many conditions surrounding priesthood as it is today. Listening to them made it clear to me that Bishop Freeman has a major task ahead of him if he believes he can entice young people into the priesthood it its present form.

Greed is Good

Greed is good; it keeps the economy stable. These were the words of a wealthy Dublin woman, explaining why she was going to vote in a certain way in a recent election. From a particular and commonly accepted point of view, she is of course correct. The more greedy people are the more they will purchase. A continued increase in the volume of purchase, or consumerism as it is usually called, is exactly what fuels the economy and keeps it stable. The more we buy the more that has to be manufactured, and the more jobs there will be.

The commentators now tell us that it was the economy that ultimately decided how people did actually vote in the last election. Not that there was any great difference between the policies on offer from the different blocks. Both of them were basically saying that they would cut taxes and increase spending on services. Maybe the good times will continue to roll, and it will actually be possible to do that, but it is doubtful. It is hard to blame politicians for offering the good times to us, the voters. Any party that campaigned on the basis of raising taxes so that real care and real opportunities could be given to the less privileged section of society would have little or no chance of getting votes in modern Ireland.

As a priest and professional preacher, the recent election highlighted for me the real task facing anyone who is trying to present the Christian message in Ireland today. When Jesus preached the kingdom of God he was presenting a view of society and human relationships which was radically different to what was prevalent in his time. To put it simply, he attempted to tell people that love made much more sense than hate, that living in peace with each other was a much happier state than war and conflict, and that there was sufficient of the goods of the world for everyone to have a decent chance at life if only we learned to share what we had, not wishing to accumulate more than we actually needed. In modern terminology, it would be fair to say that Jesus was for higher taxation, fairer taxation and redistribution. This policy for living was both simple and radical. It caused a sensation among the people, especially those who were not benefiting from the particular form of tiger prosperity that was prevalent at the time. He stirred up such fear in, and opposition from, the authorities that he was put to death. The principles on which he worked were clear. Love is good; generosity is good; selfishness and greed are bad.

I have absolutely no doubt that if Jesus was to attempt to spread that same message in modern Ireland his fate would be at least as bad, though his annihilation would be more subtle though not necessarily less barbaric. The unfortunate reality for the Christian preacher is that while greed is good and it does keep the economy stable, the values of the kingdom of God would in all probability be bad for a modern economy. If people actually began to be satisfied with what they had, and managed to control their desire to own more and more possessions, then manufacturing would inevitably begin to decline, and there would be less jobs. If people learned to live simply, appreciating and valuing the things of this world rather than wanting to possess them, the building industry, for instance, would undoubtedly suffer a downturn. In the context of living simple lives, if people began to share what they had with each other the big shopping centres, that are so much a part of modern prosperity, would suffer a serious fall in turnover. If people found something better to do on a Sunday, like going to church or walking the hills, then the long, dead-eyed queues at big department stores on Sunday afternoons would begin to shorten.

None of this, of course, will happen. We in the church have tamed the message of Jesus. We have edited it, giving an over-emphasis to matters relating to personal and sexual relationships, which he only marginally touched on, and largely ignoring the social gospel, the area where he was by far the most radical. We have recognised that this was the topic that got him into most trouble, and we have sensibly toned it down. From once his message was subsumed into institutional form, it needed to be modified for the sake of the survival of the institution. The other aspect of his teaching that ensures that it will not challenge the prevailing policy of modern Ireland is his insistence that his message was best preached by practice. Which of us is up to that?

Homosexuality and the Church

The question of homosexuality and homosexual relationships is becoming a major issue both in church and society. Commentators reckon that the fear that gay marriage might be given legal recognition was one of the factors that influenced people in America to vote for George Bush. In this country there is currently a gay couple, who were married in Canada, pursuing a case through the courts for the recognition of their union, with the privileges and tax concessions that go with it. Irish politicians who have spoken on the issue seem to be adopting a position that gay relationships deserve recognition, but that classifying them as marriages is a bridge too far for the Irish voter.

In my work as a priest I do not find it easy to uphold the church's teaching on homosexuality. My experience of homosexuals, particularly men, would suggest that many of them have a deep spiritual life, and long to give this communal expression. They have spoken about their desire to belong to the Catholic Church, but they feel condemned and rejected by us. When the church describes their orientation as an 'objective disorder', and condemns all homosexual acts as 'intrinsically evil', it is hard to expect them to feel kindly towards the church, or to be at home there. I honestly do not think it is either fair or realistic to expect all people of a homosexual orientation to remain celibate all their lives, and to refrain from any form of physical sexual expression. When this is made a condition of their belonging to the church, it is no wonder that so many walk sadly away. In the present regime, the church has taken an increasingly hard line on this. A good illustration is the case of Sr Jeanine Gramick and Fr Bob Nugent, an American nun and priest who worked for many years with the homosexual community, but who were forbidden to continue by the Vatican authorities in 1999 because they were not willing to give total external and internal adherence to the church's teaching. I imagine that many priests and religious, if we were put through a similar rigorous interrogation, would equally fail the test.

And yet the anomaly of it all is that the Catholic priesthood seems to be a profession chosen by an increasing number of gay men. Statistics on this are hard, indeed impossible, to get. The American writer Donald B. Cozzens, a former rector of a seminary, claimed in the book *The Changing Face of the Priesthood* (2002) that some seminaries in the United States had a gay population as high as 50 per cent. Around the same time an American newspaper, the *Kansas City Star* suggested that the proportionate aids death rate among Catholic priests in the States was at least four times that of the general population. It must be stated that I am not aware of any scientific basis for either of these statements.

What is the situation in the priesthood in Ireland? There are even less statistics available here. But I believe there is a perception that our seminaries (the few that are left) have a substantial number of students of homosexual orientation. It is impossible to be sure. As one student explained to me recently, students for the priesthood will do their best to hide their orientation for fear of expulsion. I understand that some of the religious orders are more open to accepting homosexuals who acknowledge their orientation than the national seminary. As I travel the country on mission work, many priests of my age-group raise with me their concern that a great many of the younger priests seem to be homosexual.

I am aware that in writing this I could be accused of being homophobic. I hope I am not. But if the priesthood has a considerably higher than average proportion of homosexuals among its ranks, is it a problem? Since all priests take a vow of celibacy, and are presumed to live their lives without any physical sexual expression, should it make any difference what orientation they are? At one level it doesn't, and I know that homosexual men are as entitled and as suited to be priests as anyone else. But it does say something about the current state of priesthood in the church. A celibate life was seen in the past as a positive thing, a witness to self-sacrifice, commitment and an unselfish availability to others. Two developments in the recent past have brought about big change in this area:

- For a long time Catholic theology barely tolerated sex, and taught that the celibate life was a higher and holier state. It does this no longer.
- The revelations of sexual abuse by some priests and religious has led people to look with a much more critical eye on the celibate life, and how it might become warped and destructive.

It would appear that heterosexual men are much less willing now to take on the celibate life involved in becoming a priest. If the priesthood consists of a majority of gay men it will, I believe, be further evidence of a dysfunctional church.

How Authority developed in the Church

The structure of government in the Catholic Church, the central position of the papacy, and how it has all developed over the years, is an interesting topic.

The first obvious point is that the system of government we have now has not been there from the beginning. In fact, after the time of Christ, the church was slow to develop any sort of centralised power system. The early Christian communities were largely independent of each other. Most of them, particularly the ones founded by St Paul, had a whole variety of ministries, operating on an equal footing; these ministries included things like preaching, teaching, prophesying, ministering to the old and sick, and of course presiding at the Eucharist. The early writings also suggest that women as well as men were active in ministry. There wasn't a central government. Decisions were made by the community. It was only slowly that the ministries began to come together into one person, who took on an authority and ministerial role resembling our present day priests. Most scholars agree that Jesus did not ordain any priests. Certainly he chose the apostles as his closest followers, and gave them authority to preach his message and to heal the sick, but to conclude that he was ordaining priests as we understand it is probably an untenable assumption. (This fact, of course, is significant in relation to the debate about the ordination of women. If Jesus did not ordain anybody, then it is not important that he did not ordain women!)

The See of the Bishop of Rome was not the central authority in the church from the beginning. In fact, it was only after the Emperor Constantine made Christianity the official religion of the Empire in the third century that Rome began to have real significance. St Augustine in the fifth century still did not recognise the authority of Rome. The Latin phrase that was used in those times about the Bishop of Rome was that he was *primus inter pares*, the first among equals. The authority of Rome over the other bishops did not become really established until the famous Hildebrand, who became Pope Gregory VII in the eleventh century. He believed strongly in the power of the papacy. His 'Dictates of the Pope' are a list of twenty-five statements about the primacy and power of the Pope. Some of them are worth quoting:

- Only the Bishop of Rome is legitimately called universal bishop.
- He alone can depose or reinstate bishops.
- He alone is permitted to decree new laws, establish new bishoprics.
- He alone may use imperial insignia.
- All rulers have to kiss the Pope's feet.
- This name is unique in the world.
- He is permitted to depose emperors.
- He himself may not be judged by anyone.
- The Roman Church has never erred, and according to the testimony of scripture will never ever err.

A century or so later, Pope Innocent III, who became Pope in 1198, went even further in terms of papal power and authority. In his sermon on the day of his consecration he described himself 'as the representative of Christ set between God and human beings, below God and above human beings, less than God and more than human beings, judge of all and to be judged by no one, except the Lord'.

By this stage it is clear that the Popes had to some extent lost the run of themselves, and become overly concerned with their own power. It is hard to imagine Jesus, who was so definite in turning his back on power of all types, and who wanted to be the servant of all, adopting these attitudes.

These two major figures inaugurated the era of the Primacy of the Pope. It reached a further highpoint when the Pope was declared infallible at the First Vatican Council in the middle of the nineteenth century. In terms of the Catholic Church's relationship with other Christian churches, both of the West and the East, those two doctrines, the primacy of the Pope and his infallibility, have been deeply divisive. But maybe even more problematic is the notion that the church cannot err. It obviously has erred many times down through the centuries. Popes have done wrong, and made very poor decisions. But to this day the church is slow to admit this, except for one or two instances where it has expressed regret over things done many centuries ago, for instance the inquisition. An organisation that believes it cannot err runs the risk of arrogance, and also a failure to learn important lessons. Those who are open learn most from their mistakes. As a church we need to make a clean break from an arrogant authoritarianism, which was clearly a feature of our past, and develop a greater degree of humility.

Influx of Foreign Nationals

Three Lithuanians are building a cut-stone wall outside a new house in Laragh, a small village in the middle of County Galway. Laragh is where I was born and reared. It was a quiet, remote little place in my youth and, if we knew about Lithuania at all, our awareness didn't go beyond believing that it was a little, insignificant state in what we were told was the evil empire of Soviet Communism. It would have been impossible for them to come to Ireland then, since travel outside the Soviet Union was forbidden, and even if they had arrived we would probably have received them with not a little suspicion and distrust, as we did any other outsider that ventured into our closed rural society. Work was scarce in those days, and the locals cherished and hoarded what they could get. But now there is plenty of work, and the Lithuanians seem to be welcome in the village, as other people who want to have the mandatory cut-stone wall built outside their new house are calling for their services.

A few days ago I said a Mass for a group of about thirty first year secondary school students from Galway, who were on retreat here in the Esker youth village. There were twelve different nationalities among them. When I asked during the Mass if there was anyone from a country that is suffering at the moment, one girl told us she was from Pakistan. If I could judge by the short period I spent with that class, they seemed to be mixing very nicely. Certainly the foreign nationals were in no way inhibited. If anything they were brighter and more forthcoming that the native Irish students.

The influx of foreign nationals into Ireland must be one of the greatest challenges this country has faced in the course of our history. We are a small nation, and the presence of so many, from such a wide spread of cultures and beliefs, is going to bring radical change to our society.

I am not sure if by nature we Irish are a particularly tolerant people. We are friendly, certainly, especially to visitors. Despite our notoriously volatile weather, we have a thriving tourist industry that depends for much of its appeal on our natural friendliness and volubility. But tolerance of people who come to live among us is a different matter entirely. Our record in other countries, especially Britain and the United States, is not good. Both those countries welcomed a great number of Irish people over the centuries, and gave them a home. Mostly they started at the bottom of the pile, and took on the hardest and most menial work. Many of our ancestors dug out the tunnels for the underground and sewers of London, for instance. But when they made money, and got themselves up the social ladder, they very often became more racist and intolerant than the indigenous population of the country.

So far it seems to me that we may not be doing too badly in relation to the current big influx of foreigners to our land. Our recent years of extraordinary prosperity have helped us. It meant that there is work available for many of those who came. Often it was work that the newly prosperous natives were no longer willing to do, either because it was not well enough paid, or because of its menial nature. So we were glad to see people coming from outside to staff our hotels, restaurants and nursing homes, and to do a lot of the heavy manual labour jobs like building walls. There have been some notable examples of exploitation of foreign workers, who were being paid less than half what native workers were getting for the same job. The fact that these people were willing to work for this wage, and maybe even consider it good because it was larger than they could earn in their own country, did not justify the exploitation.

I am not sure that I understand the State's position on work visas. Around where I live, here in the West of Ireland, there are a great number of Brazilians. These are generally hard-working, industrious people who cause little or no trouble. Until recently there was plenty of work for them to do, and they were in great demand for building, landscaping, house cleaning, and other tasks. It seems that the authorities have an ambivalent attitude towards them. On the one hand, they appear to be miserly in the provision of work visas, but on the other hand they easily turn a blind eye to the reality that many of them are actually working. I would like to see work permits more easily obtained by people who are willing to work, and when there is ample work available. But now, with the decline in the economy, and particularly what seems to be a spectacular collapse in the building industry, we are facing into a new and more difficult situation. Our attitude to the foreigners who are living among us will now be put to a much greater test.

I welcome the influx of foreign nationals into our country. I hope that we will be able to rise to the challenge of changing from a largely rural and simple society into a complex multi-cultural one without too much difficulty.

My Hope for the Church

Redemptorists have always had a special interest in moral theology, the study of the Christian teaching on human attitudes and behaviour. This is mainly due to the fact that our founder, St Alphonsus Liguori, was one of the foremost moral theologians of his time. Following in his footsteps, the great moral theologian of the twentieth century was a German Redemptorist, Bernard Häring, who died at an advanced age in 1998. His two great works, *The Law of Christ* (1954) and *Free and Faithful in Christ* (1979) were immensely influential. These could hardly be considered light reading, but Häring's last book, *My Hope for the Church*, written the year before he died, is by contrast very readable and accessible even to those who have never read theology.

It is partly a summary of his life and his work. He lived through enormously interesting times, both in church and society. He played a big part in the Second Vatican Council, and later served on the commission set up to advise the Pope on the issue of contraception. His was probably the main voice in the majority report which recommended change. As we know, Pope Paul VI went with the minority group (one of whom was Karol Wojtyla), and produced *Humanae Vitae*. Häring suggests that the motive behind the minority report was that it would be a mistake for the Pope to contradict the earlier encyclical of Pius XI, *Casti Connubii*, (1930) which banned artificial contraception. Popes should not be seen to disagree with one another. Häring describes it as 'a tragic decision. How much pain the church would have been spared if people in Rome had finally given up the hard line.'

We all know there was considerable change in the church as a result of the Vatican Council. Häring asserts that the biggest change was in the church's understanding of moral theology. For hundreds of years, church teaching had been very legalistic. The moral books contained detailed lists of sins, all graded by degree as mortal or venial. Those of us of the older generation remember those lists well, and how they affected the practice of confession. The two areas that had the longest lists were the sixth commandment and ritual, meaning the proper celebration of the Mass and the other sacraments. The change consisted in taking the emphasis off the list, and on to the person, and that person's basic attitude towards God. It was no longer the action and how the moral books defined it that decided the degree of sin. Instead the action was judged in the context of the fundamental direction of the person's life. Was the person genuinely trying to live his or her life according to the example and teaching of Christ? He is very critical of the fear factor in the legalistic style of morality, the way that so many things were classified as mortal sins, carrying with them the threat of eternal punishment in hell. He gives an example. The Congregation for Divine Worship decreed that if a priest was saying Mass and no male was available to serve, a woman could say the responses, but only from an appropriate distance: 'All authors unanimously teach that women, including nuns, are forbidden under pain of mortal sin to serve at the altar.' It is a good illustration of the type of trivial things that were classified as mortal sins.

I was particularly struck by what he had to say about the use of fear in religion.

> In almost all religions, including Catholicism, there was and still is a temptation to use the potent motive of fear, forcing people to toe the line in religion and other things. It is a satanic notion to exploit the name of God and Christ to make people submissive through feelings of anxiety, even if this exploitation is for noble causes.

I have never come across anyone who has put the case against using fear in religious teaching so strongly. He goes on:

> Add to that fear the massive threat of eternal punishment in hell for every more or less voluntary trespass, and a tremendous, paralysing potential for anxiety might develop. But, beyond that, all the available attention of Christians was fascinated and monopolised by this multitude of menacing laws and bans. In the end there was scarcely any creative energy left for constructive, liberating, and healing action.

Our emphasis all the time, he says, should be on salvation, and not just on the salvation of the individual person, which he classifies as a selfish motive for good living, ('those who think only of their own freedom are and remain slaves of egoism') but the salvation of all humanity.

I'm sure it's obvious I have enjoyed this book. If you want to know more (he has lots to say on other big issues for the church today, like priesthood and the position of women) you might get the book for yourself.

Lay People and the Vatican

I am thinking of a priest in his early seventies. He is running a large town parish, with a population of close to ten thousand people, mostly comprising the poorer area of the town. He has had a series of curates. First there were some younger men, but they found the going tough and one after the other they left the ministry. Now there are no longer any young men available in his diocese, so he depends on semi-retired foreign missionaries. These are men of about the same age as himself. They tend to come and spend a few months, or maybe a year or two, there. At their age they are great to come at all. Some of them have bad health, and all of them have spent their most energetic years in some foreign land. They do the best they can, but they are not really able to take either the burden of work or responsibility off the shoulders of the parish priest. This man is part of a generation of Irish priests who were admirable in many ways. He is dedicated, hard-working and committed. Taking days off is a foreign concept to him; he slips out once or twice a week to the local golf course, and apart from that he is on the job. He would love to be able to ease off at this time in life, maybe move to some small country parish as a curate. But he knows that option is no longer available to him. He must stay where he is and try to keep the show on the road.

This priest is an intelligent man. Even though he was trained in the old theology, which did not recognise any role for lay people in the church beyond attending Mass and doing what they were told, he has been able to read the signs of the times. He has recognised that, unless the people of the parish get more actively involved with the church and gradually assume most of the functions of the priest, the future doesn't look good. A church that depends totally on the clergy cannot survive if clergy cease to exist, or are so few in numbers that they cannot look after all the parishes. So this man has drawn a great many of his parishioners into the running of the parish. He has his pastoral council, his liturgy group (with some exceptionally talented and creative people), and a long list of ministers, both of the Word and the Eucharist. They tend to gather in the sacristy, before and after Mass. There are men and women. They are some of the nicest people you could ever meet. It is obvious that they have great time for their parish priest. But most of all they are committed to the church – they love it and very much want it to survive and thrive into the future, both for their own sakes and that of their children. Meeting these people did my heart good. They created a sense of warmth around the church, and the Mass became a real celebration of community.

And then I read the latest Vatican document, with a long list of regulations about the celebration of the Eucharist. It says that Eucharistic ministers must not be seen to be taking over the work of the priest, that they can only be used where there is no priest available. If a visiting priest is present, they must stand aside. It also says that no non-ordained person is allowed to preach at Mass. And it puts strict limitations on any type of creative liturgy, which is in practice another way of keeping non-ordained people in their place.

These types of regulations make no sense to me at all. The great hope for the Irish church is the large number of dedicated people who have gathered around their priest in every parish in Ireland where the priest is wise enough to let them. They are surely the ones who will oversee the transition to the new style of church that will have to come into being when there are only a handful of priests. And yet the Vatican wants to push them aside, to downgrade them, and emphasise that they are only laypeople, without the power of ordination. As if the basic sacrament was ordination, and not baptism. What they need is encouragement, not all these regulations telling them what they cannot do.

My hope is that the Irish bishops will ignore these regulations, and continue not just to allow, but to encourage and support, all the people who are involved with their church, and doing great work for their parish.

Lighting a Candle

This morning here in Esker where I live a large truck has just arrived with four big pallets of candles for our upcoming missions and novenas. People love lighting candles in church, and even with the obvious decline in religious practice around the country, this particular expression of faith has not diminished in any way. In fact, it seems to be becoming more popular by the day. In our missions and novenas, whenever we set up a shrine in the church, and make candles available for lighting, there is enormous demand for them. It seems to be also true that the bigger the candles, the more people like them. The most popular candles we have are ones with a picture of the Mother of Perpetual Help on the case, and that light for two days. In some of our big novenas there can be thousands of candles lighting around the church at the same time. The job of looking after these candles, lighting them, quenching them, and generally making sure they are safe, is now one of the main tasks of any large novena.

There is something very attractive and satisfying about lighting a candle in a church. Because of my love for hill-walking I have travelled extensively around the mountain regions of France, both the Pyrenees and the Alps, over the years. These regions are dotted with little hamlets down in the valleys between the mountains. They are invariably communities that have existed for many hundreds of years. Often, because of their remoteness, they have been to some extent bypassed by the changes and turmoil of the centuries. A village square is their main feature, and the dominant building in the square is an old church. In most cases these churches are no longer frequented very much, as the French have largely given up the practice of their faith. So they can have a neglected, somewhat mouldy feel to them. But no matter what time you visit them, there is invariably a candelabra in front of some shrine or other, and a few candles lighting at it. The people of the village may not go to Mass, but clearly many of them still like to slip in to the church and light their candle. It is a tall, slim white candle, maybe up to a foot long, that they use there. I always light one, and feel as I walk out that I have left a little prayer shining away for the day.

Symbols are an important part of the Christian faith. In our sacraments we use ordinary things of life, water, oil, bread, wine, a white garment. And we believe that by using them in the sacrament they take on a new and wonderful meaning. It is the human way of trying to access the deep mysteries that we believe are taking place in the sacraments. These simple things of life, things that we use and are comfortable with in our daily living, are used as gateways, as means of access to the mystery. It is the same with the candle. The lighted candle is one of the most ancient and revered symbols of Christianity. It is a sign or symbol of the risen Christ, the light of the world. 'I am the light of the world; whoever follows me will never walk in darkness.' So by lighting the candle we are doing two things. We have an intention for which we light the candle, somebody sick or in trouble, and we are praying for assistance. But we are also making a statement of our faith in the fact that Christ is not just a historical person who lived two thousand years ago, but that he is alive and present with us today. In fact, this is the most central and essential teaching of our faith. It is the core belief on which everything else stands. If Christ is not risen, alive and present with us in the world today, then all aspects of our faith lose their meaning. So there is a sense in which lighting a candle in a religious context is one of the most significant faith-filled actions we can perform.

I know that candles can be dangerous, and that fires have been caused in churches by the careless use of a candle. For this reason, and through pressure from insurance companies, many churches have replaced the ordinary candles with electronic ones. I can understand why they might do this, but I think it is a pity. In fact, I would go so far as to say that if we cannot have real live candles, we should not have candles at all. I have never felt the remotest urge to light an electronic candle. The artificiality of it is a barrier to its function as a custodian of the mystery. So I hope that, in spite of the possible risks, and taking all due precautions, we will continue the practice of lighting real candles in our churches.

My Mother's Dying

'I can see the goose!'

These words were spoken by my sister, whom I never knew. She died, at the age of three, a few years before I was born. It was back in the nineteen forties. The Second World War was still raging, and neither medical help nor transport were freely available. My mother always believed that she should not have died; that it was a simple problem she had, if the right medicine had been available at the right time. And the fact that she was her first born surely made her special in my mother's eyes.

When she herself was dying, a few years ago, at the age of almost ninety, my mother talked a lot about that first child. She mostly told simple, everyday stories from those years; recalling them with a vividness that contrasted with her dramatic loss of memory about recent events and people. The story of the missing goose, and how the little child had come running in to tell her that it had been found, was one of them.

But not all the conundrums that faced her in those last days were as easily solved as the one about the goose. Though she spent much of the time dwelling in the past, she had her lucid moments. And they were dangerous times for me, sitting by the bed. She was, in a sense, gazing into eternity, into that mist that surrounds our death, and trying to lift the veil. Just as we do in the church in the month of November, the time set aside for special remembering of our dead. An appropriate month for dwelling on such things, since all of nature is proclaiming the immutable fact that in this world everything has a life span, and must ultimately decay and die.

'Tell me,' she said suddenly one day, after a long period of rambling in the past, 'do you believe in the next life?'

Both myself and my sister, who were mainly attending to her in those last weeks, had resolved that we would try to speak truthfully, that we would resist the temptation to cover over the reality of what was happening to her, or to give simple answers to difficult questions.

'I think so,' I replied.

'What will it be like?'

It would have been easy from my perspective of relative youth and health to say that this was an impossible question, that we humans were not given a vision of eternity. But I knew that would be inadequate, because for her the question had a relevance and an immediacy that gave it the urgency I detected in her voice. It was important to her. She knew she had to go there very soon. I did not answer for a long time, and I could feel her eyes boring into me.

'You should know,' she said. 'After all, you are a priest.'

'I don't,' I said. 'I believe that it will be good; that it will surpass all our expectations. But beyond that, I know nothing.'

This time the long silence was from her, and I wondered had her mind once again drifted off. I almost hoped it had. She had become such a tiny woman, sitting up in the large bed, wondering what was ahead of her. It seemed too big a question for someone so frail and old. I anxiously searched her face for signs of fear. To my relief I could find none. Just wonderment.

'It is such a puzzle,' she said. 'Some day I must sit down and try to work it all out.'

And with that she settled back on to the pillow and closed her eyes.

Ninety years in this world, and the puzzle remained. She went into eternity a few days later, still with that sense of wonderment; still not knowing what was ahead of her. But as far as I could see she was not afraid. She trusted. Whatever awaited her, she would embrace it as she had embraced life. And she believed it would embrace her, and welcome her. Maybe that is as much as any of us can do in the face of death. Maybe it is enough.

During the month of November we Catholics remember and pray for our dead. God grant us the courage to turn away from the simplistic answers, and try to engage even in a small way with the mystery of life, death and eternity. We might even struggle to acknowledge the reality of our own approaching death, and begin to embrace with wonderment, and without fear, the amazing journey that is ahead of us.

Preparing Children for the Sacraments

May, being an appropriate time for the celebration of youth and beauty, is the most popular month for First Communions. But I discovered that even in early February the windows of the lace shops in Bruges (if you have been to Bruges you will know that every second shop sells beautiful hand-made lace) were displaying First Communion dresses. We are obviously not the only country that has commercialised this particular sacrament. But I suspect we have done a more effective job on it than most. A journalist I know explained to me recently how he would have to cut his holiday short by a day to be home for his grandchild's big day. The drinks, he said, would be in the golf club, followed by a meal in an exclusive restaurant. I wonder what would St Paul, who fulminated against the abuses at the Eucharistic celebrations in the early church where people ate and drank too much and did not share, would have to say about all this.

There is an enormous change about to happen in relation to the initiation of our children into the three sacraments of Penance, Eucharist and Confirmation in the Catholic Church in Ireland. For a long time we in the church have depended on the local primary schools to do the bulk of the work for us, with the degree of input from the priest varying according to the circumstances and the aptitude of the individual cleric. It has to be acknowledged that, in general, the schools have done a really good job, and the church owes them a great debt of gratitude. In my work I travel around the country giving missions in parishes, and invariably that involves a visit to the primary schools. Even today, at a time when the church is on the defensive and so many of the generation of young parents don't attend any more, I am constantly impressed by the dedication and commitment of the teachers in their efforts to pass on the rudiments of the faith to the children. When little or no religion is being taught in the home they are fighting an uphill battle, but they persevere. I hear criticism from certain church people, lay and clerical, about the failure of religious education in the schools. I always think that is unfair. I am amazed at how much is being done, and how well.

But already the principals of primary schools have begun to

raise questions about preparing children for the sacraments in the context of the school. They are suggesting that this is no longer a feasible idea in our modern schools where there can be a great variety of nationalities and beliefs, and indeed some children with no religious belief at all. Acknowledging that we have a Catholic school system, they have no problem with time being given to instruction in the faith, but preparation for the sacraments should, they feel, be done in a different context, independent of the school. It is hard to disagree with them.

If this were to happen, and inevitably it will sooner or later, it would mean that the church would have to create a new structure, parish based, that would cover sacramental preparation for those three sacraments. This would immediately solve one problem that is becoming increasingly difficult. In a school context there is pressure from all sides to ensure that every Catholic in the class receives the sacrament, irrespective of whether they or their parents have any interest in either faith or church. Making the preparations in the parish context, independent of the school, and done outside of school hours, would mean that only those who are committed would get involved, and the others would naturally fall away, without creating any of the sort of embarrassment that this issue is causing today.

Who would do the preparation? A generation ago there would have been plenty of nuns and brothers to do it. They are no longer available. Neither would the small number of elderly priests who struggle to staff our parishes be able to cope with this new responsibility. It would have to be taken on by the lay people of the parish. That is potentially a very interesting and exciting development. It would demand of the Irish lay Catholic that they be willing to show their commitment to their faith in a way that has never been asked of them before. In my view, that would be very healthy.

I know that there have already been some developments in this area, like the *Faith Friends* programme. And I am also aware that one or two dioceses are attempting experiments that, while involving the school, are parish based. This is good. But we will probably be forced by circumstances to move more quickly on this one. I would love to see the church becoming proactive, recognising the long-term value of parish-based programmes, and actively moving towards them, rather than waiting until the teacher's organisations or the Department of Education force our hands and decide that preparation for the sacraments is no longer appropriate in schools.

Protesting the War in Iraq

Having been a university student in Galway in the late sixties, I was familiar with protest marches. That was the era of marches, and of student activism. So we protested over student issues, over the lack of rights in many different areas of life – we even took part in a march to get the Dunkellin River drained. I can still remember the look of total consternation on my father's face the time my brother, who was student leader in UCG, as it was then, led a civil rights march to Dublin. The intention was to join up with a similar march from Queen's University, led by Bernadette Devlin and, I think, either Eamon McCann or Michael Farrell. Everything was going fine, and the Galway students were somewhere in the midlands, when the northern group crossed the border into the Republic. They immediately issued a statement calling for contraception and divorce in the South. My father was appalled that his son was involved in a direct challenge to the Catholic Church, when two more of his sons were studying for the priesthood.

For most of my adult life, I wasn't involved in any march or protest movement. But in the spring of 2003 I was shaken out of my passivity by the threat of an American invasion of Iraq, and I headed to Shannon to join one of the marches that were taking place at the time. We gathered in the town centre one Saturday morning. The march was led by Richard Boyd-Barrett and Joe Higgins. I wouldn't have been a political supporter of either, but at the time the protests against the proposed invasion were drawing in people from all strands of Irish life. It is one thing marching along as a student, chanting and singing. It is another thing altogether doing it as a grey-haired almost sixty-year-old. There was a large crowd and we began to move towards the airport. Some people had loud hailers, and they led us in various chants.

'No war in Iraq, no blood for oil, no American soldiers on our soil' was the most common one. A bit more frivolous, but easier to chant, was 'George Bush we know you; your daddy was a killer too!' I entered into the spirit of it, and after getting over an initial feeling of strangeness, was glad to be there, because I was both outraged and frightened at what the US government intended to do. A large force of Gardaí stopped us well short of the airport, so a meeting was held, some speeches were made, and we quietly dispersed and began to make our own way back to our cars. On the way back myself and a friend who accompanied me decided to drop into a local hotel for a cup of coffee. We were refused entry!

All our protests came to nothing, and the American invasion went ahead. Now, four or five years later, most people would agree that it has not been a success. Reports suggest that the country is in a worse state than it ever was, with enormous numbers of people being killed, the basic structures of society having collapsed, and even essential services like water and sanitation no longer working.

And yet we have effectively supported all this by allowing the American army free use of Shannon airport. To what extent, and for what purpose, they have used it remains largely unknown. I don't think our government really wants to know. But Shannon has undoubtedly been an instrument in the war effort. The government does not appear to have made any objection, or done anything to prevent its use. It seems to me that this has been done for a very simple reason, and that is economics. In the nineteen nineties up to three hundred companies came and set up business in this country. They did so because of our location as a member of the European Community, our tax regime, and our young, well-educated work force. And so the Celtic Tiger was born. Most of these companies were American. Around the time that America invaded Iraq, and for the first year or two of the war, there was an extraordinary outburst of patriotism in the United States. I visited America a couple of times during those years and witnessed at first hand the fervour of support for the war. This was very evident in their opposition to France, the European country who took the strongest stance against the war. I believe that our government took a very practical decision. To object to the war, and particularly the American use of Shannon, would have run the risk of some of these companies pulling out of Ireland. This could have serious effects on our economy. Since prosperity is the ultimate objective, nothing could be allowed to put it in jeopardy. And so, despite some bland and ultimately meaningless public statements to the contrary, we have in fact supported a war that is now clearly seen to be unjust, oppressive, and resulting in the destruction of a society and the death of countless thousands of people. And the voice of protest is almost silent. Even the Green Party has now become complicit. What price prosperity? What price power?

Religion is not Dead

As I write this I am part of a team giving a parish mission. We have a couple of hundred people attending early morning Masses each day of the week, a full church at night with singing and atmosphere of a type that draws people in and gets them enthusiastic, and over thirty teenagers volunteering to help at presenting the youth night. This is not in a supposedly backward little parish in the West of Ireland, but in Leinster where many people are up at an unearthly hour to commute to Dublin for their day's work. Every day as I read the papers I am told that religion is dead. Today's *Irish Times* featured a family who have developed a secular ritual to welcome their new child into the world now that the Catholic ritual of baptism is no longer relevant to their lives.

I am an avid reader of newspapers, and follow closely the current affairs programmes, listening to and reading the people who are regarded as the sharp and intelligent commentators on modern Irish life. And all the while I travel up and down the country doing my work as a preacher, and meeting untold numbers of people. I am constantly struck by the fact that so much of what I read and hear is far removed from the reality I am meeting. Not just in terms of numbers going to church, but more so in terms of the type of attitudes that are prevalent. The general impression portrayed by commentators is of a people angry, disillusioned and seriously alienated from the church. While I meet a small amount of that, what I mostly meet is warmth, friendliness and great support from people, coupled with an amazing amount of faith and courage in face of the struggles and difficulties of life. I am not suggesting that there aren't problems in the church. There are, and plenty. Attendance is declining surely. But I would have a strong impression that the decline is halting, and that a strong core is developing who will weather the storm. People come and talk to me about the shortage of priests, and what can be done about it. This current parish I am working in is being served by a priest who will be seventy later this year. He is a marvellous man, but even he cannot go on forever. I get seriously frustrated by the lack of leadership on this issue by our own church leaders, and of course the unwillingness of the Vatican to countenance any new thinking on ministry. These and other problems remain, but the situation regarding belief and religious practice around the country is nothing like as bleak as the commentators seem to suggest.

I try to work out in my mind why the national media present a picture so different to what I experience each day. Somebody drew an analogy for me with political commentators. Very often they seemed to seriously misread the mood of the people, and election results turn out very different to what they had predicted. I asked someone who is well up in political circles to explain it to me. He suggested that too many of the political commentators are reluctant to leave their offices and the comfortable confines of their Dublin environs to really find out what is happening in the country. So often what we get from them is not so much what people think, but what they themselves believe that people should think. He would even suggest that there is a degree of arrogance in some commentators that gives them an almost Messiah like complex, turning them into preachers in the dogmatic style of the Old Testament prophets.

Maybe that is a harsh assessment, and it is certainly not true of all the social commentators we have in Ireland today, but I do think there is enough truth in it to explain some of the anomalies that I am experiencing. I have wondered for some time would religious belief and practice in Ireland go the same way as the continent of Europe. I feared it would. Now I am inclined to be more optimistic. I think that there is a great opportunity for a renewed and vibrant church. Enough people are remaining faithful through all the difficulties, and there is a growing awareness that material prosperity does not have the answer to the fundamental questions of life. It is still all to play for. But the official church needs to grasp the opportunity with energy and enthusiasm to match that of the people. That is where I have doubts. Can we, the people in leadership in our church, rise above our timidity? Can we stop looking over our shoulder at what the Vatican might say, stop worrying about whether we are transgressing rules and regulations that no longer have any relevance, and go forward with open minds and hearts to let loose the Spirit that is present in the people? History judges most harshly the ones who fail for lack of courage. Let us pray that will not be our fate.

Saving Hay

The month of June used to be a great time for saving hay. I wonder how many of my readers ever saved hay. It was very much a feature of my youth. I grew up on a small farm. Since my father worked in the local Bord na Móna bog, farming was only a part-time activity. We never got mechanised, so all our hay-making was done with hand instruments, forks and rakes. My father was one of the mildest of men, who kept his emotions strictly under control. The only time I can remember him really losing his cool was when there was a field of hay cut and in need of saving, and a threat of rain. There was always a threat of rain. In those days the weather forecasts weren't quite as dependable as they are now, and even when they promised a few dry sunny days he wasn't inclined to believe them. So for those few days he became something of a tyrant.

We children were fanatics for hurling, and June was also a great time of the year for games. Sunday could see a clash between a match and the hay. One of my memories is of myself as a young fellow reluctantly and sullenly heading for the hayfield while I could hear the hurlers in action in the sports field nearby. Our farm, situated in the middle of County Galway, was on a height where we had a clear view of the hills of south Galway and north Clare. We knew that the rain was coming when the hills were no longer visible. That was when the real panic set in, and the rush to get the hay secure before it got wet. In one of Patrick Kavanagh's poems, he uses the image of a 'flooded hay field' to describe the sadness of a particular person's face. There was nothing worse than hay that had already been saved getting a bad wetting. It was almost impossible to dry it again, and even if dried for the second time its food value was greatly diminished.

I look back now with gratitude to those days in the hayfield. I think I learned a lot from them. I learned the beautiful smell of a field of saved hay that is such a contrast to the strong, pungent smell of modern silage pits. And even the smell of a cut lawn still brings back to me the memory of long summer days.

I also learned that sometimes in life, no matter how hard we try, we are not in control. If the hay was not saved and the rain blew in from the hills, there was nothing at all we could do except put the forks and rakes over our shoulders and head for home. Then, a day or two later when the weather cleared, we had to return and make the best of a bad situation. Many times I have had to do the same in different situations in life.

I also learned a great lesson about the interconnectedness of everything in nature. The reason my father got excited when the hay was cut was that he knew the food for the animals depended on getting it saved properly. Without a good supply of hay, the animals would go hungry the following winter; the cows would not produce as much milk; their calves would be malnourished and in greater danger of being lost; and the younger animals would not fatten up for the sales, with a consequent drop in income. Without a plentiful supply of milk the family would suffer. Milk from an undernourished cow has very little cream content, and isn't much good for making butter. One of my big treats as a child was to drink a mug of buttermilk, the remains of the churning, after an evening hurling. To insure that supply, we needed to save the hay. So I learned that a failure in one aspect of the food chain in nature could have far-reaching consequences. That lesson has helped me to understand how much destruction our modern lifestyle has caused to so many species of animals, birds and plants.

But most of all I think I learned about silence. A hay field, with maybe three or four people working with traditional hand implements on a summer's evening had a particular quality of silence. Despite the hard work, and my own youth, I can still remember the peace that used sometimes settle on all of us. And that peace permeated the entire scene, dispelling any tensions that the missed hurling match may have ignited among the work force. There was a sense of closeness to nature, of oneness with all there is, that is almost impossible to find in our modern world. In June, I think of my father and the hayfield.

Self-Absorbed Prayer

It may well be the case for many people, but it certainly is true for me that, as I get older, I find that both life and God get more complex and harder to understand.

I recently had occasion to go into hospital for a medical test. There were a number of people having the same test, and afterwards we were all lying on beds in little cubicles surrounded by curtains. The specialist was coming around to give each of us our results. Thankfully his visit to me was very brief. I was fine, so I could dress and go home. But as I was basking in my sense of relief, and buttoning up my shirt, I could hear him speaking to the person in the next cubicle. There the story was very different. Clearly the man was in serious trouble, and had to face the prospect of a long series of medical treatments, with no guarantee of a successful outcome. I was struck by how quickly the perspective on life had changed radically for two people lying in adjacent cubicles. I could go out and chat with people in the waiting room about the bad summer, the world cup, or some other equally insignificant topic. My life once again stretched out ahead of me. I could ring my friends and tell them I was well. For my neighbour, on the other hand, everything was now coloured by one crucial question. Would he live or would he die?

I conduct a fair number of novenas each year. People are invited to write out their petitions and thanksgivings. They usually do it with great enthusiasm.

Dear Mother of Perpetual Help, I thank you from the bottom of my heart. I have been having treatment for cancer. After my operation I had twelve weeks of chemotherapy. Now the doctors tell me there is no sign of cancer, and I have got the all clear. I know this happened through your intercession, and the goodness of God. Thank you.

This is a fairly typical letter of thanksgiving that we receive. I have often read them out, and invited the congregation to share in the rejoicing of the person who had written it, and to join in thanking God. Would I now write something similar for myself? But as I thought about it, all I could focus on was the voice of the specialist speaking sombrely to the man next to me. He wouldn't be writing a letter of thanksgiving. Why was it me who had got the good news, while he had the sword held over his head? Was it right for me to rejoice in my good health, while he was sick? Even though I didn't know his name.

I recalled a sentence from a book I had read. 'If I was God, I would spit at Kuhn's prayer.' This is a quote from Primo Levi, from his classic autobiographical account of his time in Auschwitz, *If This Is A Man*.

It was the day of the selection, when those chosen to go to the gas chamber were picked out. Levi describes the silence that prevailed in the hut after the selection. But not everyone is silent. 'From my bunk on the top row I see and hear old Kuhn praying aloud, with his beret on his head, swaying backwards and forwards violently. Kuhn is thanking God because he has not been chosen,'

Levi is repelled and appalled by the sight of Kuhn praying. 'Does he not see Beppo the Greek in the bunk next to him, Beppo who is twenty years old and is going to the gas chamber the day after tomorrow and knows it and lies there looking fixedly at the light without saying anything and without even thinking any more?'

This is why he suggests that God might spit on Kuhn's prayer. I wonder would he equally suggest that God might spit on our prayer of thanksgiving for healing and escape from serious illness when so many others are not so lucky. I know the situation is not really similar. Levi was dealing with the work of an evil and oppressive regime. As he puts it himself:

> Does Kuhn not understand that what has happened today is an abomination, which no prayer, no pardon, no expiation by the guilty, which nothing at all in the power of man can ever clean again?

The prayer of thanksgiving at the novena is dealing, on the other hand, with the ordinary human condition, the reality of sickness and suffering. And yet there is a similarity. I suspect that God, assuming he has a universal perspective on things, must think a lot of our prayer is very selfish or, at the least, self-absorbed.

Silence

Silence is a mysterious thing. I am writing this piece on an early autumn evening in Inis Meáin, the middle and least developed of the Aran Islands. I have just gone for a walk over to Synge's chair as the sun was setting gloriously behind Inis Mór. There was so much that was remarkable about that scene, but for me the most extraordinary aspect was the silence, the complete stillness. A little while ago I was in Dachau, the former concentration camp near Munich, which is now a memorial centre. There too I experienced a deep silence. As I walked through the camp, there were hundreds of other people around the place, but the silence was intense. People spoke to each other, but slowly and in whispers. No voices were raised, and there was definitely no laughter. Even more extraordinary, though I had heard it said before, despite the presence of trees and flowers within the confines of what was the camp, during my visit there the birds certainly did not sing. The silence of Inis Meáin was beautiful, drawing you into wonder and awe. It made you feel good about yourself, and about the whole world. And, as is so often the case in these situations, I reached back thousands of years to the words of the psalms to find appropriate expression.

The heavens proclaim the glory of God,
The firmament shows forth the work of his hands …
No speech, no word, no voice is heard,
Yet his span extends to all the earth,
His word to the utmost bounds of the world.

The silence of Dachau, by contrast, was heavy and oppressive, eerie, almost frightening. It weighed us down, filled us with feelings of hopelessness, almost of despair. One silence lifted the spirit; the other shrivelled it up.

A couple of things stand out in my mind from Dachau. I saw the camp where the prisoners lived. There is only one left standing of the congested number that filled the open spaces. I visited the museum with all the images of what life was like there for twelve years from 1933 to it's liberation in 1945. I walked the square where they stood for hours each day as they were counted and punished.

But by far the most horrible was the building known as the crematorium, containing the gas chamber and the furnaces for burning the bodies. This was very much as it had been, with the massive furnaces lined along, each with its pallet on which the body was placed to be pushed into the flames. The gas chamber doubled up as a shower room – the faucets for water and gas are both clearly visible – so that the prisoners were never quite sure were they going for a shower or to their death.

When you visit a place like Dachau, and experience something of the awfulness of what happened, the only glimmer of hope that can be obtained is in the belief that some important lesson has been learned. Two things within the confines of the camp served to dampen that hope in me. The famous inscription, *Never Again*, written in six languages, seemed too certain to me in the context of what we know took place in the conflict situations in Eastern Europe over the past ten years or so. When that story comes to be fully told, will it rival Dachau in brutality? Down at the other end of the camp there are four religious monuments in close proximity. The Jews have one, also the Catholics, the Orthodox Christians, and the Protestants. It is amazing to see them lined up, presumably wishing to bring some spiritual message to this place of so much evil, and yet proclaiming by their very presence the type of division, bitterness and enmity that caused Dachau to happen.

The town of Dachau is a pleasant place, bustling and active on the day of my visit. It is a strongly Catholic area of Southern Germany, with many signs of the faith of the people still prominent. Only one hundred yards from the camp is a lovely wayside shrine. The church in the town is big and ornate. As I walked around it, and knelt to say a prayer, I tried to get my mind around the fact that many of the people who ran and worked in the camp were Catholics, and presumably they came on Sundays to Mass in that church. How was it possible that two such realities, which to us appear in total contradiction, coexisted comfortably, or perhaps uncomfortably, in their lives? The strangest thing of all, maybe, is that they were not savages. Many of them were cultured people, who loved beautiful music, and who would have had the same capacity to appreciate the beauty of an Inis Meáin sunset that we have. Is it equally true that each of us has the same capacity for brutality that they had?

Sport and Religion

Many people are saying that with the decline of organised religion sport is becoming the new religion.

The Nire is a small half parish in west Waterford, with a population of about five hundred people. They got to the Waterford club football final and were beaten by Stradbally in a replay. I was at the drawn game because we were beginning a mission in the parish that Sunday. Maybe the standard of football was not very high, but that did not take in any way from the excitement and intensity of the occasion. Everybody who could attend was there, and the parish priest, with an old cap on his head as he walked around the field and gave advice to the players, blended perfectly into the scene. The replay was fixed for the following Sunday, the day after the mission ended, which gave me a great opportunity to experience what sport meant to this particular little community. It was the main topic of conversation all week. It brought me back to the time many years ago when I was sixteen and my home club qualified for the county minor hurling final. Like the Nire players, we were then the centre of attention as all our neighbours discussed our prospects. We were celebrities in our local community in a way that not even a Hollywood star could be. Of course it was short lived. A bigger and stronger Oranmore team ended our dreams, and we were firmly back on *terra firma* the following morning. I also had the experience of giving a mission in another small half parish community, Caltra in Co Galway, shortly after they had won their first ever county title, and as they were already on their way to winning the All Ireland Club title. That was a sight to behold. Every house in the community was decorated with the colours, and the village was festooned with flags and banners.

In all of these cases, sport and community gelled perfectly together, and each drew strength and inspiration from the other. The team drew their support from the community, and in turn deepened the bonds between the people through their shared experience of both victory and defeat. I think that sport at its best has something significant in common with religious belief and practice.

Both need community, the coming together of the people, and they in turn deepen and enrich it. The other essential requirement of both is discipline and self-control. The Christian life has always put great emphasis on self-discipline as a means to living out the demands of the faith, and achieving the freedom that Christ came to give us. Without discipline a person's life tends to spiral out of control. The same is true of sport.

The Ryder Cup, the golf tournament between the best golfers of the United States and Europe, is at the other end of the sporting spectrum. Europe have had some facile victories in recent years, which has led to a lot of soul-searching among American golfers. One of the great golfers of the past, Jackie Burke, was vice-captain of a recent American team. In an article in the *Irish Independent* he was clearly taken aback by the men who were representing his country. His language is colourful, but what he had to say was revealing. 'When the commerce side in golf is so much bigger than the art side, you are going to get your ass handed to you.' The American players, he said, 'have never had to work hard; never had to teach golf or never had a waiter's napkin over their arm in their lives.' He depicts them as pampered and self-obsessed. They certainly weren't a team as he understood the word. 'I don't think they'd even know what you are talking about. They are very much individuals, and they hardly even speak to each other.' He contrasts their spirit to that of the European team. 'The Europeans all went home in one plane but our team went home in twelve jets.'

There could hardly be a greater contrast than that between the footballers of The Nire and the American Ryder Cup golfers. Some people suggest that is the difference between professional and amateur sport. But I don't think it is that simple. Even at the highest level of professional sport there can be sacrifice and self-discipline, great team spirit, camaraderie and the bonding together of a community of shared interest.

Sport plays an enormous part in life. I do not agree with those who negatively view it as the new religion. I believe that it promotes a healthier and happier life for the large majority of participants. I am constantly in amazement at the generosity of so many people who give endless time and energy to the training and organising of teams. I hope that sport will continue to bring joy to our lives.

The Absurdities of Life

When I was a student, making a brief and largely unsuccessful attempt to master the French language, I was particularly fascinated with Camus. His notion of the absurd was something that I wondered a great deal about. I was too young and inexperienced to understand it. Recently a friend and myself began to draw up a list of some of the absurdities of modern life. We were surprised at how easily the list came to us.

We began with the extraordinary amount of new houses being built around the country. As families get smaller, houses get bigger. The average family today has no more than two children, while the houses being built often have up to ten rooms, with maybe four or five bedrooms. Equally, as houses get more lavish and comfortable, with all possible modern conveniences, people spend less and less time in them. Because of the size of the mortgage, and because today's wife is as likely to be following a profession as her husband, it is usual that both parents are at work all day, and the baby with a child minder. So, the beautiful house, for which they will work so hard for most of their life, stands empty. Surely, this is absurd.

Equally we noticed that many of our business friends seem to be working harder, and to be under greater stress, as they move into their middle to late fifties. At a time when common sense would dictate that they begin to slow down, they are going at a faster pace than ever. For many of them there is no longer any great financial pressure, so the original reason for the hard work has disappeared. It is an absurd thing to be doing, but, like so many absurdities, people don't seem to ask themselves why. Instead they watch their diets, go to the gym, and get regular health checks, trying to prevent the heart attack that could be brought on by all the stress.

Family life today also contains many absurdities. Even though it is commonly accepted that self-control is an important quality in the living of one's life, and that it is something that needs to be taught at an early age, yet many parents shower their children with gadgets and toys, seemingly trying to meet their every need and whim, however extreme. The result could well be a generation of self-indulgent adults.

Our behaviour on the roads is another area. Death, especially of a young person, is regarded as a great tragedy, and when it happens we are plunged into grief. One of the great causes of death is road accidents. But do we take all the necessary precautions to prevent such tragedy? Absurdly, we don't. Many people still drive recklessly, often under the influence of alcohol. Many, mostly male, drivers don't wear a seat belt. And, maybe most absurd of all, despite the fact that there is a national speed limit of one hundred kilometres, and one hundred and twenty on motorways, manufacturers are making cars that can travel easily at nearly twice that speed, and are advertising them precisely on the basis of their speed and power. While we rush on our journeys, getting irritated and stressed at hold-ups along the way, very often we have nothing in particular we want to do when we get to our destination.

There are absurdities in the religious area too. People are throwing aside the Christian philosophy of life as no longer credible, and then replacing it with visits to fortune-tellers, soothsayers, astrologers, or others who have a much weaker philosophical basis for what they teach. Meanwhile in the church itself people are gazing at statues in the hope that they will move, or believing in the most wierd and extraordinary reported messages from on high. At a time of supposed enlightenment, religious insanity is increasing.

Church laws and practices can also be absurd. For many years I, and my generation of male, celibate priests, dictated to married women about the most intimate areas of their marriage relationships. At present, in the Catholic Church in England, a priest has to leave his parish, and his ministry, if he wishes to get married, and then he can be replaced by a married priest who has come over from the Anglican Church, and is allowed to minister as a Catholic priest while remaining married. For one it is a crime meriting expulsion; for the other it is no problem.

The list is endless. With all the modern means of communication there seems to be more lonliness and isolation than ever before. We are increasingly infatuated with the 'new', which ultimately means that everything we buy is already out of date by the very act of acquiring it. One could go one. Maybe you would like to make your own list. It's great fun. But when you begin to personalise it, and list the absurdities in your own life, then it gets uncomfortable. I think I should take another look at Camus.

The Abuse of Children

The Commission to Inquire into Child Abuse looked a fairly serious and formidable gathering in the brief shot on the *Nine O'Clock News* as they inquired into the treatment of children at an orphanage in Newtownforbes between 1940 and 1945. Apparently the children were poorly fed, and subject to physical abuse in those years. The Sisters of Mercy, who ran the orphanage, apologised yet again for their failures of the past. If we had enough enquiries we would discover that there was a lot of hunger, and physical abuse, suffered by the children of Ireland in those far distant war years. The stories from the orphanages could be replicated in many of the homes and schools of the time. A great deal of apologising would need to be done.

Two disturbing reports in relation to the abuse of children were made public around the same time. First we had the *Prime Time* investigation of the sex trade in Ireland. It would appear to be alive and well in most of our cities and many of the people involved are adolescent girls and boys from Eastern European countries. It made for very unpleasant viewing, and I was surprised at the limited reaction to it in the following days. The second report was in relation to personnel from various NGO and United Nations organisations working in Liberia and other African countries. Apparently some of them are exploiting the local children for sex. This report did not particularly point at Irish people in those countries, but since we are noted for the numbers of NGOs and United Nations personnel we send to Africa, I was surprised that the report did not get more notice and response here. After all we have been through in recent years, we should be sufficiently realistic to suspect that if this abuse is going on, Irish people are as likely to be involved in it as anyone else.

There are other ways in which children are neglected in modern Ireland. The lifestyle forced on many of our young parents makes it almost impossible for them to give sufficient time and attention to the rearing of their children. Because of the enormous price they have to pay for their house, they are burdened by a mortgage that makes it essential that both husband and wife continue to work outside the home, and the child is left in a crèche from early morning till late evening five days a week. What the long-term effect on our children will be can only be guessed at. Our modern lifestyle is also putting great stress on marriage. How the young generation of parents can cope with such a stressful life, and yet keep a relationship intact, is a source of amazement to me. Marriages are splitting up, and new relationships being formed. Some children have to deal with a number of different adults acting in the role of parent during their upbringing. This must be very confusing, and again its long-term effects will only become apparent later.

Today's parents are the first generation in this country who, in many instances, have the facility to give their children whatever they ask for in terms of material goods. If it is the case that they feel guilty for not spending enough time with them, there is a great temptation to shower them with possessions instead. Grandparents can be to blame also, as often they have more spending money at this time of their life than they had in the past. Indulging their grandchildren is easy and tempting for them. As a consequence children are growing up without ever coming to know how to deny themselves anything. In this they are failing to learn what is possibly the most important lesson for life, the ability to say 'no' to ourselves. How will they cope when life, as it does, presents them with situations in which they cannot have everything they want? There is a danger they will fall to pieces. The high suicide rates and the prevalence of binge drinking among our young are indications that this is happening.

The common assumption today is that the experience of sexual abuse does almost irreparable damage to a child, which will impact on their whole life. It would appear to be classified as the worst form of abuse. But can we be sure of that? How does one measure the damage done to a child by one form of neglect or abuse more than another?

Does it strike anybody else besides myself that it is a bit strange that we are devoting so much time, money and energy on enquiring into the abuse of children half a century ago when there is so much of it happening around us today? The other obvious anomaly, beginning to be highlighted by some commentators, is that all the enquiries are into the behaviour of Catholic Church institutions and people, even though their abuse, dreadful as it was, is only a tiny fraction of all the abuse of children that happened in the past.

From where I stand, it seems that we are taking the easy way out on two counts. It is much simpler to delve into the failures of the past than the present. As a society we still have an adolescent obsession with the Catholic Church, even though its traditional power has long since dissipated. It is much more fun to keep kicking the church than to face the real problems of today.

The Clerical Church

I was talking recently to a priest working in a diocese in the south of Ireland. He gave me an insight into the life of priests working in parishes that I hadn't fully appreciated before. This man is in his early forties, with nearly twenty years of priestly work behind him, both in Ireland and on the missions in Peru. He was not very sanguine about his future as a priest in the Irish church system.

He told me that his parish priest was in his mid-sixties, just a few years older than myself. 'I envy your age-group of priests,' he said. He explained that the two of them were working together in a large suburban parish, which meant that they could cover for each other, and get some time off without too many complications. 'But in twenty years' time, when I am in my sixties, I will be running one, if not two, parishes all on my own. And from what I see, the Irish Catholics will still have the same expectations in terms of service that they have now. They will still expect me to be available for every baptism, wedding (and reception), funeral, and to provide them with a choice of weekend Masses.'

During his years working in Peru he found the laity much easier to deal with. They had a tradition of a scarcity of priests, so when there was no priest available they just got on with it themselves. 'In Ireland,' he said, 'the people are spoiled after generations of a superfluity of priests. They have come to expect too much, and we are making little or no headway in educating them about the new reality that we are all facing.' He wondered if he should go back to Peru, where he believed he would have an easier old age than what appeared to be awaiting him as a priest in Ireland.

He set me thinking of an article I had just been reading. It was by John Allen, the Roman correspondent for the *National Catholic Reporter*. John was on a lecture tour in Latin America. His comments were interesting. Latin America has had five hundred years or more of Catholicism. In all those centuries, the Catholic Church experienced little or no competition from any other religion for the minds and hearts of the people. And yet, Allen observed, it is true that most of the countries of South America are riddled with corruption. He was compelled to ask the question as to why five centuries of Catholic teaching had not done more to improve that situation. The answers he got were not convincing. According to him they fell back on the old line of Chesterton that Christianity had not failed, rather it had not been tried. But that leads one to wonder what exactly the church was doing there for the last five hundred years.

Now things have changed and the position of the Catholic Church is being seriously challenged by the Evangelical Churches from North America. Allen gave the example of Honduras, where it is estimated that about one third of the population have now gone over to one or other of these churches. He told the story of one woman who was a patient in hospital. The local Catholic chaplain, who also had a large parish to run, was only able to pay her one or two fleeting visits. The evangelicals, on the other hand, were visiting her each day, bringing presents and spending time with her. This is because they are lay-centred churches with a great number of people involved in various forms of ministry. In this they are much more in line with the original style of the early Christian churches. By contrast, the Catholic Church has over the years become so dependent on the ordained ministry that it has largely side-lined the lay people. Raymond Brown, the great scripture scholar, points out that this is one of the problems of churches with an ordained ministry:

> The presence of an ordained priesthood can have the unfortunate side-effect of minimalising an appreciation of the priesthood of all believers. The ordained will frequently be assumed to be more important and automatically more holy. Because ordination is seen as a sacrament and priests deal with sacred things, they are frequently regarded as better than ordinary Christians.

This tends to create a two-tiered system where the ordained person is seen as the one who has the power to do the spiritual things, and the ordinary church member is relegated to a type of second-class citizenship, where he has no real function in ministry, and also where he can happily sit back and leave it all to the priest.

Faced with the challenge of secularism in the West, and the rise of the Evangelicals in Latin America and Africa, it seems to me that the Catholic Church is severely shackled by its overdependence on clericalism, the system of priestly ministry that the church is clinging to with an almost desperate determination.

The Death of Doris

Doris Cotteril was dying. There was no question about it. She was little more than skin and bone as she lay on the bed, and with her eyes standing out prominently from her emaciated skull, filled with a look that was both fear and wonderment. She and her husband Frank had recently moved to a town in the south of England, and two major events had coincided in her life. She had become a Catholic, after a lifetime of non-belief, and she had got seriously ill. They were both in their sixties, with no children or any relations in that part of the country. She wanted to die at home and Frank was doing his best to keep her there until the end. When I, a visiting priest in the parish, called to see them Frank, with that admirable straightness that so many English people possess, quickly informed me that he was an atheist, that he had never been a believer.

'But I'm very impressed by your people.' he went on to say. It took me a while to realise that 'your people' were the small group of Catholics who lived in this large new town, and belonged to the parish of Holy Trinity. 'Ever since Doris became a Catholic, and got sick, that door bell rings and there are people standing there who are total strangers to me. "We are from the church, and we would like to visit your wife", they say. I leave them with her; she tells me they chat and pray, and I know their visits do her a lot of good. In the last few days, now that Doris is very low and needs full-time attention, two people come each night and keep watch while I get some sleep. They are very good people.'

When Frank showed me up to Doris she wasn't able to say much, but enough to let me know that she was aware the end was near.

'Are you worried or afraid?' I asked her.

'Yes', she answered, and then, because the whole experience of being a Catholic was so new to her, she continued, 'Is it wrong for a Catholic to be afraid to die?'

I reassured her on that, and enquired if she was in pain, if she was suffering. She nodded. But then she went on to explain to me how an old woman from the parish had told her about the

Christian notion of suffering, and how her pain could be a source of blessing for others, in the same way that the suffering of Jesus has brought blessing on the whole world. 'It is easier to suffer,' she said, 'now that I know it has some meaning and purpose.'

The next day, when I called again to see Doris, she was in a coma, and she died that night.

In my experience the English are not a people who like going to funerals. I was afraid, considering that Doris and Frank had no children and no relations in the area, that her funeral would be very small. So, at the weekend Masses, as I prayed for Doris, I suggested that anyone who was free might come along to the funeral Mass on the Wednesday morning.

Frank and four companions were in position in the front seat half an hour before the funeral Mass was due to begin. Only five people to mourn Doris! They were clearly unfamiliar with church, but they were people for whom good manners and right behaviour were paramount. So they sat stiffly in the seat, with their eyes fixed firmly ahead, hardly moving a muscle. So ill at ease were they that they didn't realise the little church was filling up behind them. It was only when I came out of the sacristy to begin the Mass, and the people stood up and spontaneously began to sing a hymn, that Frank realised there were more people in the church than himself and his companions. For a matter of a few seconds he lost his sense of right behaviour. He turned in the seat, and stared around the church. His face was one big question mark. 'Who are these people? Where have they come from, and what are they doing here?' It was the Catholics, who had come to give him a bit of support as he buried his wife, and who sang and prayed with gusto for the next forty-five minutes or so.

I met Frank two weeks later. He was still overwhelmed by the whole experience, and talked incessantly about it. He summed his feelings up in the following sentence: 'Father, I've never been a believer; I've always been convinced that there was no God. But, since meeting your people, I'm not so sure anymore'.

And in that moment I came to realise the depth of meaning contained in the sentence of Jesus: 'If you have love one for another, then everyone will know that you are my disciples.'

The Dilemma facing the Catholic Church

I was asked to conduct the funeral of the mother of a friend of mine recently. It was in a city parish in the south of Ireland. When I arrived, the sacristan, now an older woman, reminded me that I had given a mission in that parish about twenty-five years ago. We chatted for a while and she told me I had predicted during that mission that the day would come when there would only be small groups of people attending church. 'We all thought you were a pessimist, but now your prediction has come true', she said in a resigned voice.

I took no pleasure in having been proved right in this instance. Big city churches with small gatherings of older people attending weekend Masses do not lift the spirit. Then I met the priest. I remembered that there had been three priests in that parish. Now he was on his own. There were four funerals that week, he told me, and he was kept going trying to keep up with the daily demands of his position. There was no way he could have either the time or the energy to develop anything new that might begin to restore life to the parish. I asked him about various priests I knew when I worked around that area. Were they still alive? Had they retired? 'Nobody retires any more in this diocese', he said. 'We must endure to the end, in order to keep the show on the road'.

Unfortunately that is increasingly the reality of priests' lives around this country. They are continuing to work hard long after the age when they should be taking it easy, in order to serve the needs of an institution that utterly refuses to look at the crisis that it is facing, and begin to think creatively about a solution. We have gone through a period of a century and a half when we produced many more priests and religious that we needed, so they went as missionaries around the world. That time has come to an end. There are many reasons for this. Families are much smaller than they used to be. Prosperity has given young people far more options than they had in the past. It has also resulted in a decline in religious belief and practice. As the poet T. S. Eliot said: 'In times of prosperity people neglect the temple.' The priesthood is no longer considered a special and honoured profession in the way it was during those years. This has partly to do with the scandals. But it has also been brought about by a dramatic change in attitudes towards sexuality. Celibacy, particularly of the compulsory type demanded by the church for its priests, is regarded by many people as somewhat inhuman and unhealthy, maybe even suspicious. Parents are no longer encouraging their sons to become priests like they did in the past.

It amazes me that church authorities do not seem to be tackling this problem with any degree of urgency. Instead they are moving their dwindling supply of priests around in order to continue as much as possible to do what was done in the past. In theory they are in favour of more involvement by the people in the life of the parish and dioceses but, despite a few honourable exceptions, little or nothing is being done. Today's women and men are reluctant to get involved in parishes where they have a purely consultative role, and the priest has all the power of decision making.

There is talk of introducing lay deacons. This would be new in the Irish church, though they have been common in other countries for many years. But this role would only be open to men, and I think that to introduce a new function within the church that would exclude women would be a disastrous move in the present climate. It would serve to highlight even more starkly the male domination of the church.

So little happens. And in the meantime the system is collapsing, and church attendance is declining. Something creative and courageous is needed to rescue us from this situation. Where will it come from? Who is the Spirit working through in the church today? Can we at least begin to talk about it?

The Enduring Nature of Humanity

My father loved the land. He had only thirty-five acres, and a lot of it was boggy and wet, but that in no way diminished his love for it. Being the younger son, he inherited nothing from home, and it must have been a great day in his life when his uncle left him his farm. I don't know if he was a very good farmer. Having been one of the founding members of the National Farmers Association in Co Galway back in the nineteen fifties, he liked to be at the fore-front of developments and experimentation. He avidly read the *Farmers' Journal* each week looking for new ideas. They weren't all a success. I can remember cutting kale with a small hatchet on cold frosty mornings, and throwing it over the hedge to the cattle, be-fore I went to school. I think we rebelled against him on that one. I know we stopped growing it, and I never wanted to see the long hard stalks again. It was just too much hardship. Neither was the chicory garden a success. It was meant to be the latest and best food for the pigs, but my memory is that the rabbits got there first. Or maybe it was the slugs. There was little enough money to be made from small farms in those days, and but for the jobs in Bord na Móna, which gave my father a second income and gave us summer work to help pay our school fees, and our mother's dressmaking, life would have been much more difficult.

None of us inherited his love for the farm, so when we got some education and other avenues opened up for us, we easily and happily turned our backs on it. When he died in his early sixties twenty-six years ago the land was leased to another farmer. I don't know if it was some deeply suppressed guilt, or respect for his memory, that kept us from selling it until a couple of years ago. Somebody bought it and got permission to build. Now when I pay a call to the old family home, which we have retained and renovated, I look out the window and I see houses being built in the land that my father cherished. A Sherry Fitzgerald magazine informs me that the guide price for these houses is three hundred thousand euro. This is a sum of money so far beyond anything my father could ever have con-ceived of, utterly beyond what might have been made from farming the land. And now half an acre can be valued at that, with a house on it. Many a time I saved hay on those half acres, using the most traditional of instruments, a fork and a rake. We watched my uncle, because it was his role to declare when the hay was sufficiently dry and saved to begin to make the cocks. I loved the sight of the first cock going up. The end of the work was in view. I also have childhood memories of bright summer mornings, with the dew glistening on the grass in that same land, watching the rabbits frolic and graze. I think of my father. It is so strange to see it now, with the big earth-moving machine ripping up the hedges and trees that he spent many days and years putting in place. This is the end of all his ambitions to be a progressive farmer. I do believe in eternity, and I believe that his spirit is still in existence. I wonder if he is aware of what is happening to his land, and if so, what does he think of it all. I feel like asking his forgiveness for what we have done. And yet I don't. Because the Ireland of the twenty-first century is such a different reality from that of the nineteen fifties. He was a man of his time who recognised the inevitability of change. He would be aware that we must move on, and part of what moving on entails is letting go of the past.

As I look out the window and the images of the past flit across my mind, I am amazed at the extraordinary upheavals my generation has experienced. We have come from the simplicity and relative poverty of a traditional rural society to the opportunity and excesses of the Celtic Tiger. I think that it is greatly to our credit that we have managed to preserve a degree of stability, and to hold on to at least some of our values. I am not of the constituency that believes the world is going to the dogs, humanly and morally more corrupt. Instead I marvel at the endurance of humanity, and how we manage to adapt and change so much in the course of our lifetime, and yet retain sufficient emotional and psychological balance to help us live reasonably good and fulfilling lives.

The future of Old Monastic Settlements

Esker Monastery, where I currently live, is an old monastic settlement that carries the aura and mystique of a place where people have gathered to pray for centuries. It has its origin in the sacking of the Dominican Abbey in Athenry in Cromwellian times. The inhabitants of the monastery fled to the most remote and desolate place they could find. That was Esker. Of course it is no longer remote and desolate, being only fifteen miles from Galway City, and the new motorway passing within half a mile of us, and with plenty of lovely new houses. We Redemptorists have been here since 1901. At one stage it was our student house, later the novitiate, and for the last forty years or so a retreat centre where people come for residential retreats. About fifteen years ago, the farm buildings were renovated and converted into what we call a Youth Village, where schools come for retreats during the year and the Chernobyl children spend a summer holiday.

The difficulty facing us, the Redemptorist Community here in Esker is twofold.

Firstly, our own numbers are declining and we are ageing. There is only one member of the community under sixty years of age. The number of new recruits for the Redemptorists is small, and there is no way that we can continue to run an establishment of this size on our own.

Our second problem is that the mainstay of the Retreat Centre has been priests and religious. They came in great numbers each year to do their annual retreat. It was a popular place, because of the silence and peace, the wooded walks, and the sense of history making it a holy place. Now, of course, priests and religious are declining in numbers, so clearly an institution that depends on that market does not have a future.

So what do we do? The easiest thing would be to gradually wind the place down and either move to one of our other monasteries or build something much smaller and more suitable to our current needs. But we are reluctant to take that option. We are constantly being told that people right around the county of Galway value Esker and love coming here. They very much want it to continue. The question is can we do that?

We are exploring our options at the moment. We already have a large staff of people working here, in the kitchen, around the house and in the office. But we also have moved into the area of lay ministry, with two full-time and two part-time lay people working in the youth village and as part of our mission team. This initiative has great potential for expansion. In the Irish church today there are many lay people who are trained in theology, liturgy or spirituality. Some go into teaching, but others are looking for openings in more direct pastoral work, and not having much success. Part of the problem is financial. If we employ a lay person in ministry we need to be able to pay them a salary that is to some degree equivalent to what they would get as a teacher or nurse. This has an immediate effect on the cost base of a retreat centre because traditionally Redemptorists worked in them for nothing, and staff wages were never a factor in balancing the budget. Luckily we are in the process of selling property in Dublin and Belfast, and hope to commit ourselves to using some of this money to employ lay people as co-workers in our ministry. The other question raised by this development is how can we preserve the unique Redemptorist message and charism if the work is being largely done by people who are not Redemptorists. There is a big challenge for us there.

The second problem is probably more difficult to solve. Can we discover new markets for what we have to offer in this place? In the absence of priests and religious, will other people be interested in coming here, and if so, what will bring them? It is often said that life today is very pressurised, and I can see from my own experience that many are suffering from stress and anxiety. People need places where they can go to get away from it all for a while, where they can be still and quiet, and find a bit of peace. We can certainly offer that. But we need to find modern, effective ways of promoting ourselves, and persuading people that a stay in Esker will do them great good, both in body and spirit. That gets us into the whole world of advertising and selling ourselves, a world that is largely unfamiliar to us, and in which we have little expertise. In this, as in so many other areas of our life and work, we will need to learn how to be in partnership with lay people. Whatever the future is going to bring, it will undoubtedly be very different from the past.

The Ordination of Women

I happen to know a few of the women who were ordained to the priesthood on a boat at the meeting of the three rivers in Pittsburgh, Pennsylvania. For those who don't know, there is a movement of women within the Catholic Church who have been ordaining some of their members to the priesthood for the last ten years or so. Around the beginning of the century three German women were consecrated bishops. They say they were validly consecrated by a Catholic bishop, whose name they will not reveal in order to protect him. Since then they have held a number of ordination ceremonies in different countries in which they ordained women. In each case the ceremony is held on a boat on a river. Their reason for this is to perform the ceremony in a location that cannot be identified with a particular diocese, so as to avoid direct conflict with an individual bishop.

The women who went through the ordination ceremony on that boat, performed by the three female bishops, were an interesting group of people. They were all of an older age group, some with children and grandchildren. Without exception they had at least a Masters degree in some aspect of theology. Also they had given many years, in some cases up to thirty, of service to the Catholic Church. Some of them had lectured in seminaries or other courses in theology; others had worked in some form of pastoral administration, others as counsellors or catechists. From that point of view they had 'walked the walk' in terms of their commitment to the faith, and indeed to the church. Why then did they decide, at this later stage in their lives, to take the step that would entail them being cut off from the church? I asked one of them, a woman who had worked for many years in adult religious education in her diocese. She explained to me that for a long time she had felt angry and hurt by what she perceived as the second class treatment of women within the church. She had lived in hope that there would be change, that at least some aspects of the official ministry of the church would be opened to women. But now she was losing hope of anything coming from the top. So she decided that the only way forward was to make a move herself. She got in touch with the movement for women's ordination, and put her name forward. She claimed that history indicated that change in the church was more likely to happen from the ground, and that by ordaining women they would show that women priests are not a cause for fear, and that the ordinary catholics would mostly accept them without any problem. She told me that there was a deep sadness in her that it had come to this. If she had been given any openings in the church for ministry, if for instance she had been allowed to become a deacon, she would have been perfectly satisfied. After her years of working in her diocese she knew the priests very well. When she let it be known that she was taking this step many of them spoke to her privately about how they understood why she was doing it, and they wished her well. But at the same time a letter went out to all branches of diocesan ministry saying that she was no longer acceptable, and neither was she to be recommended to anyone else. That she found difficult.

Of course all these women, who go through this ceremony of ordination, are put under the penalty of excommunication by the church.

I, being a man and a priest, am aware that I cannot appreciate the depth of hurt that some women feel in the Catholic Church. I recently got a letter from an American woman theologian who has taken a public stand in favour of dialogue about the ordination of women. She says that as a result she is being victimised:

> I am only allowed into Catholic colleges on condition that I agree not to talk or write about women's issues in the church. What kind of Body of Christ does the church build if over half the members are women and are under a 'gag order'? How can we share the same Eucharistic table when the human presider orders half the attendees to keep some of their deepest concerns to themselves?

She concludes by stating the women who share her beliefs and hopes 'are being treated with contempt and lack of human respect.'

I know that none of this is easy, and that the question of some form of ministerial role for women is a very controversial issue in the Catholic Church. I know that there are many who are deeply opposed to it. But I do think that dialogue is a better form of response than excommunication. And I am sad that the church is losing out on the committed service of so many women who seem to feel they can no longer stay within an institution that they believe does not grant them equality.

The Power of Books

One of the advantages of being known for writing is that every now and again people give you some of their own scribblings, and ask for your opinion on them. Some time ago a priest from a generation slightly older than myself gave me some notes he had written on his seminary training, and in particular the books that he read during those years.

He first recounts how his mother had given him *The Confessions of St Augustine* when he was sixteen, and when he brought it back with him to the boarding school the Principal of the school, a priest, took it off him, saying he was too young and that he could read it later. He reflected on that experience:

> I got a new respect for books. They were powerful, and their power needed to be controlled. In the long years of studying for the priesthood my reading was constantly monitored. I became powerfully drawn to the forbidden. I became convinced that I could learn more from the dangerous than the safe. I did not believe that I needed to be protected from books.'

Books played a major part in his life from then on.

> When I was eighteen I joined a religious order. The spiritual year came first. Secular reading in any form was not on the curriculum. We must read about God and the saints alone. As a reader, it was the most barren year of my life. The lives of the saints which we were given were written solely for the edification of the young and those of simple faith. They were an insult to both categories. In theory, spiritual literature should be the greatest literature of all. The great spiritual classics were not put into our hands. Dostoyevsky, Kafka or Simone Weil were not in our novitiate library. We were protected from any knowledge of the struggles and temptations of great souls. We were given spiritual pulp-fiction. It is the sad genius of the Catholic Church that it has produced so many boring books for the edification of the faithful!

He then goes on to talk about the seminary years that followed.

When I left the noviciate and went to the seminary, my greatest hunger was to read a good book. The first one I was given was *The Longest Day*, by Cornelius Ryan, a bestselling thriller, which I enjoyed. When an older student asked what I was reading and I told him, he said: 'I will get you a good book.' So he brought me to the library and presented me with *The Portrait of the Artist as a Young Man*, by James Joyce. It hit me with the force of Pentecost Sunday. The intellectual excitement that it aroused in my mind was as intense as a sexual awakening. It was the first time I came face to face with ideas that did not have the blessing of Mother Church. I read with intense interest about Joyce's rejection of Irish culture and the church, and his reasons for choosing exile. It filled me with happiness. It belonged to a world of great ideas and great literature.

He then goes on to talk about the topics he studied in class during those years.

We studied philosophy from an ancient Latin textbook. I found it difficult to understand, and my mind did not connect with it. To this day I am not sure what it was about. We studied the difference between essence and existence, between substance and accident. We were learning the thinking of the ancient Greek philosophers. Thomas Aquinas had used their insights into the nature of matter to make sense of some aspects of theology, especially the Eucharist. I found it all mind-numbing. One evening towards the end of class our teacher wrote a sentence on the board:

'If God does not exist, there is only one question, whether or not to commit suicide.'

It caught my attention. It was my first introduction to existentialism. A light came on in the darkness. I could grapple with this question, and discuss it endlessly with my friends. Some time later I discovered that it was a quote from the great French philosopher, Albert Camus. By then I had fallen in love with the passionate clarity of Camus' thinking. I valued his freedom from all ideologies. I was overawed by his Christ-like love of humanity. 'If I had to choose between justice and my mother, I would choose my mother,' he wrote at a time in history when countless millions were being slaughtered in the name of fascism, communism, and other versions of justice. I could see in his thinking the mind of Christ.

I had found a philosophy I could love. After class, each day, I went to the library. There I found something that refreshed me from the boredom of the official textbooks. I never found out who stocked the library with so many modern classics. Whoever he was, may God bless his enlightened soul.

I don't know if modern seminary education engages the students more than it did this man about fifty years ago. I hope it does. But I also hope they find time for some of what he describes as the great spiritual classics.

The Problem of Loneliness

One day last summer, at a clergy golf tournament, a priest I used to know asked me if I was writing anything at the moment. I explained what I was doing. Then he said: 'Why don't you write about loneliness? When I go home tonight I won't even have a cat to welcome me.'

He is the sole priest in his parish, living in a big old house out the country. Clearly the isolation of his situation is difficult for him. I suggested that maybe it was a topic he should attempt to write about himself. But he did set me thinking.

Not long afterwards I met an American Episcopalian nun who was visiting Ireland. In the course of a chat over a bite to eat, she asked me if I ever had regrets about becoming a priest. I explained that at this stage of my life I did miss not having children, and maybe even more so, grandchildren. I see people of my age, I told her, and I am acutely aware of how their lives are brightened and engaged by the generations coming after them. I know enough about life to know that families aren't always a bundle of joy, and are also capable of bringing great sorrow and unhappiness. But nevertheless, I said, I am conscious of a certain emptiness.

Loneliness is not the preserve of celibate religious and priests. To a greater or lesser extent it is part of everyone's life. I can remember spending two hours listening to a young married man as he talked about how his marriage was collapsing around him, despite his desperate attempts to save it. I could see that the space he was occupying at that moment was immensely lonely, even desolate.

I spoke on the phone to a woman in her fifties, single and living out the country. She was suffering from depression, partly brought on by the isolation of her life. The degree of loneliness she seemed to be suffering was far greater than anything I have experienced, or indeed would want to experience.

In his novel *When We Were Orphans*, the writer Kazuo Ishiguro puts an interesting slant on the whole problem of loneliness. The main character, Christopher, is invited by Sarah, who is leaving a hopeless marriage, to go off with her. He objects that he cannot, because his work is too important, he has a crucial mission that he needs to fulfil. Her answer goes like this:

'Oh, Christopher, we're both as bad as each other. We've got to stop thinking like that. Otherwise there'll be nothing for either of us, just more of what we've had all these years. Just more loneliness, more days with nothing in our lives except some whatever-it-is telling us we haven't done enough yet. We have to put that all behind us now.'

He says it's too late, but she objects:

'All I know is that I've wasted all these years looking for some-thing, a sort of trophy I'd get only if I really, really did enough to deserve it. But I don't want it any more. I want something else now, something warm and sheltering, something I can turn to, regardless of what I do, regardless of who I become. Something that will be there always, like tomorrow's sky.'

When I read that it rang bells for me, especially the bit about our lives being dominated by 'whatever-it-is telling us we haven't done enough yet'. Many of my generation entered religious life and priesthood with a great sense of mission, that we were given a voc-ation, and it was incumbent on us to live up to it. So we were in a sense driven people. There is a very positive aspect to that. Driven people tend to be the ones who achieve a lot in life. But they can be left with a sense of purposelessness in the end. In the last chapter, Christopher talks to the only person he is close to, a young adopted niece, about his ambition. 'It all amounted to very little in the end,' he tells her. That is the danger for us: that we will reach old age and look back at all the struggle and effort of life, and conclude that it was of very little significance.

This is where religious faith can help. If we believe that our lives are spent in promoting not just our own plans, but the overall plan of God for the world, it helps to give our paltry efforts significance. If we believe that God can take what is small and seemingly unim-portant, and make it into something worthwhile, we will more eas-ily find meaning and purpose. Some people say that a close, personal relationship with God can protect them from loneliness. This may be true, though the lives of the saints indicate that in such cases God can distance himself and seemingly leave a person to struggle on their own, the 'dark night of the soul' as John of the Cross called it.

For most of us the greatest bulwark against loneliness is other people. That is what Sarah meant when she said what she looked for now was 'something warm and sheltering, something I can turn to, regardless of what I do, regardless of who I become'. Christopher didn't go with her. He stayed with his ambition. I wonder if he had gone, would he still have concluded that it 'amounted to very little in the end'.

The Problem of Suicide

When I was a young priest I was called out of the monastery one day to attend a man who had committed suicide. It was my first experience of suicide. At the time he was a member of what was regarded as the group most at risk – a man in his fifties, a farmer, single and living alone in an old house at the end of a boreen. He was lonely and depressed. He hanged himself in the shed.

Nowadays, suicide has become much more common than it was thirty years ago, even if in those times it tended to be hidden, and the profile of the group most a risk is very different. It is still more likely to be a male, (though increasingly girls are also doing it) but he will probably be much younger, in his late teens or twenties, and could come from any social class or any profession.

Most of us are baffled as to why this is happening. In some cases there are apparent reasons, like conflict or depression, but in an increasing number of instances it seems to come out of the blue, as if it was an impulsive act born of a moment of desperation. There is some anecdotal evidence that suggests that many cases of suicide are related to high consumption of alcohol, but I am not aware that there are any statistics on this.

In the past, the act of suicide brought with it strong social and religious sanctions. The person was refused the rituals of the church and buried in unconsecrated ground. It was regarded as a major disgrace on the family. As a consequence, suicide was hardly ever mentioned, and if it was possible the death would be attributed to some other cause. Now all that has changed. If the suicide is a young person, the funeral tends to be an enormous event, with great displays of emotion and overstated eulogies. Does this lead other young people to see it as an option? If you are in your teens, with a poor self image and a life that seems to be going nowhere, it might be tempting to choose an option that would send you out in a blaze of glory. From our perspective, the attitudes of the past seem to be harsh. They were certainly that, but is it possible that they were also more realistic, and based on a clearer understanding of the weakness and frailty of the human person and of the need for social constraints to hold our lives together?

Whatever the myriad contributory factors for suicide, it would appear to me that the act makes one clear statement, that the person, at least temporarily, has lost any sense of meaning in his/her life. A reading of Tolstoy's *Anna Karenina* presented me again with the question of life's meaning.

Towards the end of the book Levin, one of the central characters, has rediscovered his faith. He reflects on the change it will make in his life:

'I shall still get angry with Ivan the coachman in the same way, shall dispute in the same way, shall inappropriately express my thoughts; there will still be a wall between my soul's holy of holies and other people; even my wife I shall still blame for my own fears and shall repent of it. My reason will still not understand why I pray, but I shall still pray; and my life, my whole life, independently of anything that may happen to me, is every moment of it no longer meaningless as it was before, but has an unquestionable meaning of goodness with which I have the power to invest it.'

I love that phrase 'an unquestionable meaning of goodness'. That is the great bulwark against despair, depression and suicide. If a person can recognise that their whole life is invested with meaning, including the sad, tragic and unhappy things, then they will be less likely to end it of their own hand. With Levin it was the rediscovery of his faith that gave him that meaning.

The Christian faith tells us that we have a God who is passionately concerned for us, and who wishes to work out his plan for our happiness through all the circumstances of our lives. I have no doubt that the increasing incidence of suicide among our young people is connected to the decline in religious faith. A belief in a faithful God who gives an unquestionable meaning of goodness to our lives is a much more solid bulwark against meaninglessness than most of what today's young Irish people place their faith in. A classic study on suicide by Durkheim suggests that when society is in transition and when the old shared values break down (arguably what is happening in today's Ireland), that suicide becomes common.

Professionals tell us we need more investment in counselling and support services. I'm sure that will be some help, but it will be equivalent to keeping out the tide with a fork unless we can give our young people a philosophical and religious basis that will give some meaning to their lives. We might consider Italy – there philosophy is a subject for students at second level.

What is the Purpose of Education?

I gave up teaching in my mid-twenties after a short and, if I am to be honest, relatively undistinguished career. I am now becoming aware that my contemporaries are either retired, or looking forward to imminent retirement, with a good financial package available to them. Unfortunately, in the profession I choose instead, there is little facility for retirement. Once a priest, always a priest! Winding down a little in your mid-seventies might be tolerated, but with the current shortage of priests, there are some who are working away in parishes even into their eighties. Maybe they are as well off.

I did enjoy my few years in front of a class, but I was always conscious of the somewhat contradictory forces that were at work in the education system, making it difficult for me to know what exactly my purpose and goals as a teacher were. I think that the contradictions that I refer to are even more obvious today than they were then, thirty-five years ago, when there was less pressure around exams, and points were what we got in football or hurling games.

This came home to me shortly after the Leaving Cert results came out in August, when I heard the Minister for Education, Mary Hannifin, encouraging students who had got their Leaving Cert results to consider studying science subjects at third level. I presume her motivation in making this call was that market forces are dictating that we need more science graduates to serve the needs of the economy. Everybody tells us that one of the big reasons for the success of the Celtic Tiger was the availability of so many highly skilled young graduates. When I did my Higher Diploma in Education in Mary Immaculate College in Limerick under Fr Jim Good all those years ago, we were introduced to the ancient Greek philosophers who taught that the purpose of education was to develop the whole person to his or her full potential. I think it is fair to say that the marketplace is not particularly interested in a fully rounded human being so much as someone who has the specific skills for the job that needs to be done. The demands of the market place have a much more dominant voice in deciding education policy now than they had in my teaching days. A good example is the relegation of the study of history to an optional subject for senior years. I would put history, along with literature and languages, at the centre of any educational curriculum for young people. In my way of looking at things, learning how to cope with ourselves and our lives, and how to be a positive member of society, are ultimately much more important lessons than the skills needed to make big money in our modern enterprises.

Something of the same dilemma is present in religious education. If you are a teacher of religious education in a Catholic school is it your purpose to guide your students into becoming good believing Catholics? Or instead, should you try to give them the broadest possible understanding of the spiritual dimension of life, and a basic knowledge of all the major religions, and then trust that they will decide for themselves what, if anything, they will believe in? I came across an interesting conflict around these two different approaches in a school recently. There were a series of modules in the curriculum, but with a degree of choice about which ones would be taught. One catechist, who saw her function as passing on the Catholic faith, suggested that the module on other world religions could be omitted. The other catechist, who felt that the students' minds needed to be broadened so that they could make more informed choices, considered the module on world religions to be possibly the most important of all. They had two very different understandings of their function as religious educators in a Catholic school.

I was impressed by a speech of Enda Kenny calling for a national debate on the values and standards that should characterise the future of our country. He hopes that this debate will help us, as a society, to build a moral consciousness, an ethical consciousness based on our shared values, our rights and our responsibilities.

He said:

'There is a great need to protect our children, and the shrinking space of their childhood. As a father and a politician I have grave and growing concern about the early sexualisation of our young teenagers, whom I consider to be children.

Progress alone has not brought with it the necessary prosperity of mind, prosperity of spirit. For all our success, so many of us, especially our young people, are Grand Canyon deep in psychic pain.'

In the time of the Greek Philosophers, it was the great teachers who were leading this type of debate. I would love to see our third level institutions become centres of discussion on these issues again.

The Promise is Life, not Death

The many and various forms of religious expression that I meet still have the power to surprise, and sometimes appal me. I find myself wondering what sort of warped and perverted mentalities some people must have to persuade them to believe what they do. I was recently on a mission in Lisdoonvarna. The season had just ended, and there were still some visitors in the town. One of them was an Englishman who proceeded to favour me with various typed A4 pages, each instalment getting more lurid than the previous one. After two days of this, he informed me that he was leaving town, and that while he would give me his final document he would advise me not to read it, because I might find it too upsetting. It was a document predicting that the large majority, indeed over 95% of people, were destined for hell. To back up his argument he had numerous quotations from saints down through the ages. It interested, but did not surprise me, to note that the most frequently quoted saint was our own St Alphonsus!

Thankfully I have long ago dealt with the fear of hell in my own life, and it is no longer a significant part of my religious belief. But this man clearly was getting some pleasure and satisfaction out of spreading his news. He was not unique. In my years of ministry I have met many like him, and have been told of plenty of 'visionaries' who proclaim a somewhat similar message. To do it in a Christian context makes no sense whatever. If God created humanity in order to condemn the large majority of them to hell, the only conclusion we could come to would be that God was a nasty, vindictive tyrant who took pleasure in the pain of others. Definitely not a God of love! A God like that would not be worth believing in, and he would deserve neither honour nor respect from human beings. Heaven would not be a desirable destination. To be living for all eternity with a God of such viciousness and callous indifference to the sufferings of others would surely not constitute happiness. Hell would then undoubtedly become the better option, because it would be the only place in which people might have a chance of spreading some love.

In other words, to present the Christian message as saying that hell is the destiny of the majority of people is utterly preposterous, and an insult and profanity to the God that Jesus Christ presented as our Father.

Theologians tell us that hell exists, in the sense of being a place that is separated from the love of God. But the church has never said that anyone has gone there. We certainly hope not.

I got the perfect antidote to my hell-promoting gentleman when I went the following week to *Uncle Vanya*, a Checkov play adapted by Brian Friel, at the Gate Theatre. It is about a dysfunctional family. At the end only Vanya and his niece Sonya are left on stage. Vanya curls himself up like a ball on the sofa and tells Sonya how unhappy he is, and asks her what they can do. Everything has fallen apart. She sits beside him, puts her arm around his shoulder, and tells him (as accurately as I can remember it): 'What we must do is endure, keep on living and keep on working. And when our time comes to die we will face that too. We will say to God that we have done our best. And a great wave of mercy and compassion will sweep over us, the stars will shine in the sky like diamonds for us, and we will be at peace. We will look back on our lives, with all the misery and unhappiness, and we will smile.'

That is a message worth preaching, something worth proclaiming in front of a church full of people. I am now thirty-five years preaching, and I am more convinced than ever that if I haven't something positive, something joyful and inspired by love, to say to the people, then I should say nothing at all. I would see no point whatsoever in threatening or frightening people, even if the result was that they would desist from doing certain things. A virtuous life lived out of the motive of fear is of no interest to me. If someone lives a cautious, fearful and risk-free life in order to ensure that they will get to heaven, it seems to me a negation of Christianity. Love always involves courage, and a willingness to take chances and risks. In fact, I think the salvation of our souls should not concern us at all, because it is fundamentally a selfish concern. Let us live our lives as fully as we can, and try to be as loving as possible, and when we come to die we too can tell God that we have done our best. And I have no doubt that the same great wave of mercy and compassion will sweep over us, and the stars will shine in the sky like diamonds for us, and we too will be at peace.

The Year of Magical Thinking

I am reading Joan Didion's *The Year of Magical Thinking*, at the moment, and I am fascinated, absorbed and at the same time slightly repelled by it. It is a wonderful book, in which the author attempts to describe the experience of the first twelve months after her husband of almost forty years died suddenly while they sat down to dinner one evening. It isn't the book that repels me. It is the awful and frightening reality of what she struggles to write about. The thought of what happened to her, and how the same thing could happen to me or to you at any moment is intensely disturbing. There are one or two people in my life, and to think that I might one day have to go on without them raises in me, not so much fear as something far stronger, a feeling of almost uncontrollable panic. It is one of these harsh realities of life that we try to push aside in the hope that it might not happen. And yet it could happen any day. To quote from Didion's book:

> Life changes fast.
> Life changes in the instant.
> You sit down to dinner and life as you know it ends.

Or the phone rings, or there is a knock at the door, and life as you know it ends.

Both her husband and herself were deeply taken by a verse from a poem of Gerard Manley Hopkins, and it becomes a central theme of the book:

> O the mind, mind has mountains; cliffs of fall
> Frightful, sheer, no-man-fathomed. Hold them cheap
> May who ne'er hung there.
> I wake and feel the fell of dark, not day.
> And I have asked to be
> Where no storms come.

I know that many of you reading this will have already experienced that moment when life as you knew it came to an end. So for you that sentence, *I wake and feel the fell of dark, not day,* will speak volumes. Surely those hours of early morning, lying in bed after a restless and unrefreshing sleep, must be the hardest. It is then that we enter into those *cliffs of fall*, the mountains of the mind where we are lost and alone.

And I have asked to be where no storms come. I am not good to pray. I have gone through many phases and stages of prayer in the course of my life, and in some ways I am worse at it now that I ever was. And yet I don't know if that is true. I recently had the experience of an urgent situation where I desperately wished for a particular outcome. I pray more easily walking than in a church or chapel. So I set out for my walk and began to ask God for that particular outcome I desired. But in the course of the walk a couple of deep realisations came to me. I stopped praying for the outcome that I wanted. I became conscious, in a deeper sense than ever before, that my years on this earth have given me an awareness of the mystery of life, a sense that it is utterly beyond anything I can fathom or understand. In the light of this mystery there is no possible way that I can know which outcome to any situation is for the best in the overall perspective of a person's life, not to mention getting some grip of what insight an eternal perspective might give. I also realised at that moment that my belief in God is very much imbued with what we called in the old days the providence of God, a belief that God is in control and that he is bringing about what is best for all of us. I would seem at this stage to have come to a largely positive understanding of God, and to have rid myself of the fears and anxieties I felt towards him in the past. So I didn't pray, like Hopkins, to be in a place where no storms come, because maybe it is the storm times that can also be the growth times in life. So my prayer as I walked along became that old prayer, Thy Will be Done, and I found some peace in the praying of it.

But maybe all this is too easy, and I am still left with a question, as I read Joan Didion and wonder what is ahead of me in my life. It is that other sentence in the Hopkins poem: *Hold them cheap may who ne'er hung there.* What is before me yet that will bring me into that mountainous region of my mind? What *cliffs of fall, Frightful, sheer, no-man-fathomed* have I yet to face in my life? And will that scrap of faith, that hard won, precious and yet fragile attachment to a caring God that I have discovered in myself be able to sustain me? I pray that it will.

Three Practical Steps
to Improve the Church

Recently somebody put this challenge to me. She asked me to suggest three practical things that the Irish church could do to improve its ministry. After some thought, I suggested the following:

When John the Baptist in prison was beginning to have doubts about Jesus, and sent a messenger to him to know if he was the one that was expected, the answer Jesus gave is very revealing: 'Go and tell John what you have heard and seen. The blind see, the lame walk, lepers are cleansed, the deaf hear, the dead are raised to life and the poor have the Good News preached to them.'

Clearly the big test of the Christian, either as individual or as community, is how we respond to the poor. In Ireland we have focused a lot of our energy in the past on getting people to practice their religion, meaning attendance at Mass and the sacraments. That has its own importance. But it wasn't the acid test laid down by Jesus. As a Catholic community we must be on the side of the poor, the marginalised, those whom society rejects. Every local community of Christian believers must have an outreach to those in need. In other words, people who are poor, a person in despair or suicidal, a young pregnant girl, a husband and wife whose marriage is in difficulty, or people in any need, would know that within the Catholic community they would find acceptance, understanding and help. That would mean creating structures, some of which are already in place. We have organisations like Cura, St Vincent de Paul and others who are doing some of this. But we need many more, and ones that are more localised, more identified with the local community of believers. About forty years ago there was a move to set up social services in some dioceses. Ossory, Killaloe and Limerick had very successful Social Service organisations, and were visible signs of the church's care for the poor. Unfortunately, as time went by these services came to rely on state funding and consequently lost their independence, being eventually largely subsumed into the state model. We need to revisit these initiatives. We could have a social service organisation in each diocese that would be funded by the diocese, locally based in the communities, and with services available to anybody in need. This would need to be owned and supported by the people, so that they would be willing to contribute what is necessary to fund it. The Catholic community would have to undergo a mind shift which accepts that contributing to such a service is as integral a part of our religion as Mass attendance. The present custom of throwing a coin into the basket at weekend Mass would have to be replaced by the contribution of a substantial donation that would be a sign of real commitment. It is one of the particular problems of the Irish church. The small contributions made by the believers were enough to support a poorly paid clergy in the past, but will be utterly inadequate to pay full time lay workers, not to mention the sort of initiative I am suggesting here. Being funded by the church and independent of the state system would give this type of social service much greater flexibility and availability. Such an initiative would be a real witness to the fact that the Christian community recognised that service to the poor is an essential part of Christian living.

The second area where I feel we could make real headway in a short space of time is in creating a church that is inclusive. By that I mean a church that is open to everyone who wishes to be a member. One of the outstanding features of the ministry of Jesus, and one that made him many enemies, was his acceptance of everybody, be they sinners, outcasts, lepers, whatever. On the other hand, the real signal that a church has developed into a sect is when they begin to exclude people, when they begin to divide the world into those who are chosen and those who are not. An inclusive church would need to send out a clear message that everyone is welcome. Nobody would be excluded, no matter what state their lives are in, or what their orientation may be. In fact, the person whose life is in a mess, or who is clearly not succeeding in living the Christian ideal, would be particularly welcome. Of course, if a person is hardened in a destructive or sinful way of life, they will not want to be part of the community. The only requirement necessary for membership would be that the person wants to belong. This will demand great openness and tolerance from the members, and an end to judgemental attitudes. One of the big temptations of religious people is to become judgemental, to begin to see themselves as better than others, and to look down in condemnation on those who appear not to be living by the same high standards as themselves. Where it occurs it is a particularly unpleasant side-effect of religious belief. It was prevalent in the time of Jesus. I know that some people will see the type of open community I am describing as a watering down of Christian moral values. They will point to the words of Jesus to the woman caught in adultery: 'Go in peace, but do not sin again.' Jesus did not use that sentence as a threat. He was not telling her that if she continued to sin she would have no business coming back to him. What he meant was that her sinful life was destructive of herself and others, and that she would only find peace when she changed and began to live by different values. That is the ideal for all Christian communities. They would not impose their values by excluding people, but rather by encouragement and good example. Sinners recognised the futility and hopelessness of their lifestyle when they came face to face with the goodness of Jesus, and they wanted to change. The same dynamic should work within the Christian community. So let's not exclude anyone. Make them welcome, and give them motivation and support in their efforts to become new and better people.

This development in pastoral practice will not come from the Vatican. The authorities there will continue to tell us that, among others, people in second relationships after their first marriage has broken up, or gay people in a sexual union, are in a state of serious sin, and cannot receive the sacraments unless they promise to give up their behaviour. We must not wait for a lead from there. The bishops could act on it. Traditionally a bishop in his own diocese had much more power and autonomy than is being exercised at present. If the Irish bishops proclaimed that all Christian communities must be inclusive and that no person would be refused membership or sacraments, there would be little or nothing that the Vatican could do about it. A unified body of bishops making a statement like that would be a wonderful message of compassion from the church. If all the Irish Bishops could not agree on this message of inclusivity, then maybe a number of them together could do so.

The third commitment that the church could make immediately is to include lay people as fully as possible in the life of the church. Already much is happening in this area, but it is uneven both in terms of policy and action. If all dioceses were to make it a cornerstone of their approach at all levels it would send out a strong message. Appointments of priests to parishes would be clearly understood as implying a willingness to work in collaboration with the local people. As the shortage of priests creates vacancies, and priests are brought in from other countries, this would be one of the conditions under which they would come. A priest coming in to a parish and disbanding the existing structures of lay involvement would no longer be tolerated. As a specific expression of this, each parish could be instructed to have a liturgy group that would be actively involved in the organisation and preparation of all Sunday Masses and other liturgical events.

I think that these three suggestions are all possible, and that they would make a great difference to the church at local level, which of course is where church is really church.

What type of God allows Tragedies to Happen?

This is a reflection on that awful tsunami in South East Asia where so many people lost their lives. Many articles were written about how we can relate this event to our understanding of God. It is a real and difficult question. We know so little about God. The Protestant theologian, Karl Barth, said that when we think about God we blaspheme, and when we speak about him we doubly blaspheme. Anthony de Mello said that any idea we have of God is more unlike him than like him. In other words, both are saying that God is too great for our puny little minds to understand. I have no problem with accepting that. I know that the mystery that is God is far beyond our understanding. And yet we do struggle with the notion of God, trying to understand something about him, and how he operates. (I am using the male pronoun 'he' applying to God for convenience sake, knowing that it is inaccurate, that females are as much in the image of God as males.)

And yet it is valid to wonder if God had any part to play in this event. Did he cause it to happen? Was it a deliberate decision on his part to set off the earthquake which caused the massive wave that put an end to so many peoples' lives? There are some who believe that he did. They interpret it as the punishment of God on a sinful and corrupt world. The fact that some of the areas most deeply affected were holiday resorts seems to confirm them in their view. Holiday resorts mean decadent lifestyles and sexual promiscuity, the sort of things that particularly anger God. I cannot accept this view for a moment. I wouldn't want to believe in a God like that.

If we conclude that God did not cause or initiate this awful event, did he passively sit by and let it happen? Could he have stopped it, but didn't? For thirty years I have preached sermons about the nature of God. Following what I understand as the message of the New Testament, I have spoken about him as a loving God, one who cares for each of us, who 'holds us in the palm of his hand'; one who always wants what is best for us, because his will is that we grow into the fullness of our being, which is his plan for everyone. This love that God has for us is faithful and unending. If I am correct in that presentation of God, then he did not either cause or passively allow these thousands of people to go to such a horrible death. Is he then almighty, and all-powerful? And if he is not, how can he be God? I will have to re-think that sermon. The reality is more complex.

The second image of God that I have presented in my missionary work was not quite so consciously done as the first one. I have worked from time to time at all the major Redemptorist solemn novenas. Along with those big events we also use the novena as an alternative form of mission in many parishes. A popular aspect of the novena is writing out petitions. We encourage people to do this as a form of prayer, and we read out a number of petitions at each session. I have become increasingly aware that these petitions encourage a particular and specific image of God. 'Dear Mother of Perpetual Help, pray to God to cure my daughter of her cancer.' 'Dear Mother, help me so that my depression will lift, and I will feel happier and more at peace in myself.' The God that we pray to in the novenas is close at hand, and is actively involved in all the little affairs of humanity. He knows about our most minor worries and ailments, and he can cure them all, if we persist in asking him. He is undoubtedly in control, and he decides what will happen. And yet it is hard to know how this type of God would allow such a terrible event.

Maybe God is not the all-powerful controller of all our lives. A remarkable aspect of this tragedy is the way people all over the world have responded so magnificently. There has been a wonderful outbreak of care and help. Is this the part that God is playing? Maybe he is the spirit of love and goodness that inspires people at a time like this. Could he be the one who suffers rather than the one who controls?

But if the last judgement turns out to be like we have traditionally imagined, with God totting up our individual ledgers and deciding on our destiny, then we too might have some questions to ask of him.

Will the Poor always be with us?

There were a few Sundays during the autumn this year when the gospel dealt with the social teaching of Jesus. It is striking that he was much stronger on this topic than on others. He told the rich young man to sell all that he possessed; another rich man was condemned to eternal torment because he ignored Lazarus, the poor man, at his gate; in the last judgement scene we hear: 'Depart from me into the everlasting fire … because I was hungry and you did not feed me …'

It is probably not surprising that Christians down through the centuries have had difficulty with this part of the teaching of Jesus. The fastest growing branch of Christianity today, Protestant Evangelism, especially of the American variety, tends to quietly put it aside. Some of them even revert to an Old Testament notion that wealth is a sign of God's blessing, and poverty is a punishment for sin.

In the Catholic Church we have had differences of opinion also. The church authorities are very comfortable with Mother Teresa's style of working for the poor. As we know, she and her sisters engaged with them at a very basic level, going out into the streets of Calcutta and taking in the totally destitute. By any estimate, this is admirable work, and is surely putting the gospel message into practice. Mother Teresa is well on her way to canonisation.

But I think it is fair to say that neither Mother Teresa nor her followers ever engaged in the task of trying to change the structures and systems that were creating poverty in the first place. The church in South America attempted to do this some years ago. They too were dealing with societies in which there was great inequality and extreme poverty. Through the movement that eventually came to be known as Liberation Theology, they began to bring the poor people together to read the gospel and reflect on their situation in the light of what it said. This led to criticism of the corrupt systems of power that were causing poverty. Gradually the movement began to agitate for change, and allied itself with other groups, like socialists and communists, that had similar aims. The church authorities, cautious by nature, got very uncomfortable with this, and cracked down on the movement. They were afraid of political upheaval. They silenced some of the leading thinkers behind it, most notably the theologian Leonardo Boff. I think this was a great pity. I am not suggesting that their approach was better than that of Mother Teresa, but there should surely be a place for both in the church. After all, the Chief Priest accused Jesus of being a political agitator.

When we bring the question of social justice home to our own country it is also complicated. Is there poverty in Ireland? Charlie McCreevy, in his years as Minister for Finance, often claimed that he had largely eliminated poverty. He used say that a rising tide would lift all boats, and that the years of the Celtic tiger had brought prosperity to all. Others, like Fr Seán Healy of CORI and the Combat Poverty agency claim that at least a quarter of our people live in poverty, meaning that they do not have sufficient income to live a decent life. The structures created around the wealthy block the poor people from access to the means of achieving some prosperity for themselves. Picking up on the McCreevy image, they say that the rising tide lifted the yachts of the well-off but left the boats of the poor stuck in the mud of the harbour. In his address to the Fianna Fáil party, Healy called for the state to pay a living wage to every person. In order to pay for this the well off would have to contribute higher taxes. The following Sunday McCreevy rubbished this idea, dismissing it as an old nineteen sixties socialist pipedream that would ruin the economy with high taxation. Instead of giving the poor a better standard of life, he asserted it would bring us all back to the old days of unemployment and emigration. Imagine an Irish politician campaigning on the platform of higher taxation of the wealthy in order to give money to the poor. I don't think he or she would get many votes. There is a perception that we are becoming an increasingly selfish and uncaring society.

There are no easy answers in all of this. And yet Jesus had very strong things to say about it. If we take our faith seriously we must allow ourselves to be constantly challenged by the Christian obligation to be on the side of the poor and the deprived, in a way that impacts on our own lives. If we ignore the poor people at the gate, either in national or world terms, we may suffer the condemnation of the rich man in the gospel.

Young People and the Faith
*(This articles was written about seven years ago,
hence the reference to George Best)*

During a mission in Dublin city I found myself, one afternoon, addressing a group of about twenty-five fifth year students in a local secondary school. They were lovely, in the sense that they were well-behaved, attentive, and they gradually became quite responsive as they overcame their initial reticence. At fifty-four years of age, and having been in religious life since the middle sixties, I now find myself somewhat uncertain when attempting to talk to young people. What I am uncertain about is what to say, and even more so the problem of language. The language we use, and the meaning it carries, is so much influenced by our background and experience. And my background and experience is fairly radically different to the average young person of today.

So when they began to find their tongues I was able to relax. Happily they have lost the fear of clergy that previous generations had, and seem to have no problem about speaking openly. They told me about their attitudes to church-going. They go to weddings, they said, and occasionally to funerals; baptisms, particularly of members of the family, also brought them along. Apart from that, the only other time that most of them went to church was at Christmas.

I considered that baptisms, wedding and funeral were easy to understand, as they are major family events. Christmas seemed somewhat different. 'Why do you go at Christmas?' I asked. 'Because we'd feel guilty if we didn't' was the surprising answer. I thought I was dealing with a generation for whom guilt was no more than a folk memory. When I asked them why they do not go to Mass more regularly I got the very predictable answer that it was boring.

It is when I get to this point in my discussion with young people that I wonder what I should say, what line is best to take in order to get through to them. How can these young people be convinced that they should give another chance to organised religion? As it happened I was listening to *Liveline*, Joe Duffy's programme on RTÉ, as I drove to the school and they were discussing George Best, and his drink problem. I didn't expect these young girls to know who George Best was, but they were very familiar with him, and his story. (Not every fifty-four year old was irrelevant to them!) On the programme, a number of callers rang in suggesting that the only hope George had was to turn to God, to hand the problem over to him. I told the students this, and went on to suggest that unless we have something to give meaning to our lives we will not be able to cope when things get difficult. Unless we have somebody to turn to when our backs are to the wall we will be in serious trouble. I was conscious of stares that could well be interpreted as blank, or maybe a 'we heard all that before' look.

I decided to change my line of argument. There were a number of non-nationals, mostly Africans, in the group, and I could see from the few comments they made that their attitude to their religion was different. Most of them seemed to be committed to regular attendance at Sunday Mass, and had no difficulty with it. I asked them were they surprised at the attitude to religion they found among their contemporaries in Ireland. 'Very surprised,' the most talkative one said. She had expected to find people who were deeply Catholic, and proud of it. 'Why was that?' some of her Irish classmates wanted to know. She explained that in Africa they had been given the faith by Irish nuns and priests, and now she wondered what had happened to make Ireland change so much. 'I was surprised to find that there were more pubs than churches,' she said, 'and that it is in the pubs the people spend their time.' Being deliberately provocative, I said to the young students, 'So, you see, you are the first generation in this country to lose your faith.' Their response was vehement. 'Just because we don't go to Mass doesn't mean we've lost our faith. We still believe, and say our prayers.' This time it was my turn not to be impressed, to put on that 'I've heard it all before' look. I suggested that, even if they didn't completely lose their faith, their children certainly would; that faith cannot survive without the support of a community coming together to pray and to celebrate.

At this point we had almost come to the end of the class period. I finished by explaining to them about our mission, and inviting them to come along. In particular I asked them to get involved in the night dedicated to young people. They smiled politely at me. But that night, when I looked around for them at the mission, and more especially at the meeting afterwards to prepare the youth night, not one of them was to be seen. And yet I have no doubt that the Christian message has something of crucial importance to say to them. So the struggle to communicate must continue.

Young People and Sex

Recently a friend put a challenge to me. 'If you were speaking to a group of young people on the subject of sexuality, and you could only say one thing to them, what would it be? Could you encapsulate it into one sentence?'

I responded straight away that it would be unlikely that I would find myself in that situation; that there was a time when I spoke a fair bit about sexuality, but not any more.

'Is that because of the scandals?' he asked.

I answered that it wasn't really, though maybe they were a factor in it. It had to do more with a sense that the general track record of the church in this area wasn't particularly distinguished. I told him a story:

> I was chatting with an old man, sitting in a seat of the church in a West of Ireland town. He looked over at one of the confessionals, which were still the same as they had been sixty years ago, when he was in his late teens. He was going with a girl at the time. He explained to me that 'going with a girl' in the early nineteen forties, in that particular area, meant going for walks to the next village a mile down the coast. He assured me he hadn't even got as far as kissing her. But when the missioners came to the town and he went to confession, all his training told him that he should feel guilty about even something as innocent as he was engaged in, so he confessed that he was 'company-keeping'. He was roundly abused, and warned that unless he promised to stop seeing the girl he would not be given absolution. Since the particular style of confession box in that church tended to amplify, rather than subdue, the voice, he said that one of the hardest things he ever had to do in his life was to face out of that box, knowing that the large queue outside had heard every word of the raised voice of the missioner.

Stories like that, and they are numerous, bring home to me how daft a lot of the traditional Catholic attitudes to sex and relationships were, and that we, who came out of that era, have, despite our best efforts, been inevitably tainted by that type of thinking. So, if the younger generation have a different value system in the area of sexuality, and they have, are we in a position either to blame them or preach at them?

But my friend wasn't going to let me away that easily. 'I accept what you say,' he said. 'But, my question remains.'

A long silence developed between us, both of us deep in thought. While the situation he was putting to me was unreal, I could see the value of trying to condense your beliefs to one sentence.

'I would tell them that sex is a serious business.'

I went on to explain that I thought there was a lot that was good about young people's attitudes to sex. I envied them their freedom from oppressive guilt. But the big danger for them is that they will see sex as entertainment, as fun, maybe even as a way of passing the evening. So many of the attitudes to sex that are prevalent in the media see it in this light. And it would seem to me to be true that where people use sex just for entertainment, or fun, it can become very destructive. I have always been impressed by what Norman Mailer wrote, in an essay years ago, about how sex so often disappoints the young because of its troubling tendency to want to become something more, to transcend itself into love, or power, or destruction. In other words, there doesn't seem to me to be such a thing as recreational sex, or sex for fun. No matter what form it is engaged in, a sexual relationship is a serious matter.

So, if I could get young people to see that it is serious, and that it needs to be handled with great care and caution, then I would feel that I had gone a fair distance with them. After that I would be happy enough to trust their good judgement and common sense to work out the details of it for themselves. No doubt they will make mistakes, and some very damaging ones. But so did the generations that have gone before them. Though we often wish to do so, we of the older generation should never try to protect the young from the essential process of learning through experience.